W9-ANY-056

DISCARD
WITHDRAWAL

FIRST
IN WAR

FIRST
IN WAR

George Washington in
the American Revolution

JOHN ROSENBURG

The Millbrook Press • Brookfield, Connecticut

To the Caimes, Fraziers, Gersbachs, Jongeneels, and my wonderful wife, Rosemarie—for the sustenance.

Photographs courtesy of Brown Brothers: p. 6; Independence National Historic Park Collection: pp. 37, 138, 150; The Granger Collection, New York: p. 47; North Wind Picture Archives: pp. 61, 205; Miriam and Ira D. Wallach Division of Arts, Prints and Photographs, The New York Public Library, Astor, Lenox and Tilden Foundations: pp.65 (Eno Collection), 84 (Portrait File); Culver Pictures: pp. 119, 207, 247; The Valley Forge Historical Society: p. 143; Library of Congress: p. 192; National Archives: p. 230.

Maps on pp. 26, 71, 88, 92, 121, 227 are from *George Washington in the American Revolution* by James T. Flexner. Copyright © 1967 by James Thomas Flexner. By permission of Little, Brown and Company.

Library of Congress Cataloging-in-Publication Data
Rosenburg, John M.
First in war: George Washington in the American Revolution/John Rosenburg.
p. cm.
Includes bibliographical references (p.).
Summary: Chronicles George Washington's role in the American Revolution, from his appointment as commander in chief of the Continental Army to the British surrender at Yorktown and his famous farewell address.

ISBN 0-7613-0311-1 (lib. bdg.)
1. Washington, George. 1732–1799—Juvenile literature.
2. Generals—United States—Biography—Juvenile literature.
3. Washington, George, 1732–1799—Military leadership—Juvenile literature.   4. United States—History—Revolution, 1775–1783—Campaigns—Juvenile literature. [1. Washington, George, 1732–1799. 2. United States—History—Revolution, 1775–1783—Campaigns. 3. Generals. 4. Presidents.]
I. Title.
E312.25.R67   1998
973.3'092—dc21   97-34012   CIP   AC

Published by The Millbrook Press, Inc.
2 Old New Milford Road
Brookfield, Connecticut 06804

 *Contents*

Part One

Part Two

George Washington, commander in chief of the Continental Army.

Part One

Early on, it was his size that attracted the attention of those from the North who didn't know him.

This was not surprising since he stood at roughly six feet three inches and his reddish-brown hair, prominent nose, and calm, gray-blue eyes seemed to tower above the average American, whose height in the eighteenth century was only about five feet seven inches.

Other characteristics made a lasting first impression, too. Despite his large head, feet, and hands, his carriage was always erect. And when he walked, danced, or rode a horse, he was so graceful that every move seemed effortless.

In the Second Continental Congress—as in the First—the newly acquainted soon discovered many other admirable traits embodied by Virginia's most prominent delegate.

It was quickly noted, for example, that he was exceedingly patient and polite and not given to tiresome oratory or bombast. When he spoke, everyone within earshot listened.

"He's a practical man," one delegate said knowingly. "And when he has something to say, which isn't often, he always talks sense."

Sometimes this Virginian didn't have to speak to make a point. Tired of the endless opposition from those who still believed in reconciliation, for instance, he suddenly appeared one day in the blue-and-buff uniform he had worn in the French and Indian War seventeen years earlier. "Let's stop talking and get ready to fight," his uniform seemed to say.

Of course, the southern delegations knew all about forty-three-year-old "Colonel" George Washington. He was, after all, a military hero in their part of the country.

And during the long nights in the taverns after dinner, the southerners delighted in telling their northern neighbors about Washington's exploits on the frontier and as an aide-de-camp to British Generals Edward Braddock and John Forbes during campaigns against the French in the struggle for control of the Ohio River valley.

There was some exaggeration, of course. Be that as it may, in early June 1775, Washington's sensitive ears picked up several comments that made him uneasy.

Singly, or in twos, threes, and fours, in carriages or on horseback, they began arriving in Philadelphia early in May 1775.

While some were from Pennsylvania and nearby New Jersey and Delaware, others had traveled hundreds of miles, crossing rivers, mountains, and lakes at their own expense and in all kinds of weather.

The thirteen colonies they came from embraced an enormous area of some 200,000 square miles. Scattered thinly about this vast domain, however, was a population of only about 2,200,000, including both blacks and whites.

Philadelphia was by far the largest city, with some 34,000 residents. New York was next, with 22,000, followed by Boston and Charleston with 15,000 and 12,000 respectively.

Fifty-five delegates finally gathered in Philadelphia for the Second Continental Congress in what later became known as Independence Hall. In addition to George Washington, they included such distinguished men as John and Samuel Adams, John Hancock, John Jay, Patrick Henry, Benjamin Franklin, and Thomas Jefferson.

When called to order on May 10, these delegates had but one purpose: to convince King George III and his ministers that a ten-year assault on their rights as British subjects must be halted.

In their view, the Colonies had suffered greatly; they had been unfairly taxed and, through the passage of several laws known as the Coercive Acts, were being severely punished for standing up for their rights.

British troops had also crossed the Atlantic and invaded the Colonies, seized and occupied the major city of Boston, confiscated their powder and arms at various locations, and killed and wounded their citizens during several confrontations, including one that had become known as the Boston Massacre.

Congress had hardly begun its work, however, when an express rider from the north burst into the main meeting room with a startling bit of news: "We have captured Ti!" he shouted exultantly.

Amidst the hubbub that followed, the delegates learned that under the joint command of Benedict Arnold of Connecticut and Ethan Allen of New Hampshire, some two hundred Patriots had indeed captured a small British garrison located near Ticonderoga, New York, close to the Canadian border—and without a shot being fired!

For the delegates, the implication of this development was clear: The Patriots had gone from defense to offense, worsening an already dangerous situation.

Moving quickly, Congress sent a message to the king and his ministers: "We mean not to dissolve that union which has so long and so happily subsisted between us. We have not raised armies with ambitious designes of separation from Great Britain, and establishing independent states. We fight not for glory or conquest. . .[but] we are reduced to the alternative of choosing an unconditional submission to the tyranny of irritated ministers, or resistance by force. The latter is our choice."

Resistance by force? To many, that could mean only one thing: War.

When President John Hancock gaveled Congress to order on June 14, John Adams was the first to speak. As always, the fiery Adams, a short, muscular man in his early forties, got right to the point.

"Mr. President," he said solemnly, "Dr. Benjamin Church, a member of the Massachusetts Provincial Congress, arrived this morning with a request that we adopt the soldiers now facing the British Army in Boston and form a 'Colonial' Army."

As Adams paused, the hall buzzed with excitement. But it grew quiet as he spoke again.

"Time is running out!" he growled. "If we do not move immediately to support the New Englanders who so bravely and unselfishly continue to defend our rights against a common enemy they will become discouraged and go home.

"And why should they not? Why should they remain in the field—without pay, or sufficient food and supplies—if New England's sister colonies refuse to commit to the cause which they so loudly claim to espouse?

"And if they leave the field, what then? You know the answer! Before a new army can be raised, the British will be free to march out of Boston and lay desolation to the land wherever they care to go.

"Gentlemen, if you treasure your liberty, now is the time to establish an army that will represent all of British America!"

In the same rush of words, Adams turned quickly to Hancock and said in a different, almost angry tone, "Mr. President, as requested by Massachusetts, I move that this body promptly adopt the army now besieging Boston!"

Before Hancock could say a word, Samuel Adams jumped to his feet and, with his squeaky voice at a high pitch, said, "I second the motion!"

The delegates roared their approval, leaving no doubt about the outcome of the vote. And when it was cast, John Hancock banged his gavel and called, "Recess!"

As the members of Congress spilled out into Chestnut Street, a troubled George Washington approached Edmund Pendleton, a young lawyer who was a close friend and fellow delegate from Virginia.

"Edmund," he said, his voice kept low so others couldn't hear, "I need to talk to you. Can you join me for dinner?"

Pendleton, a handsome, brilliant man with black hair and sharp blue eyes, was not surprised by the invitation. "Of course," he said quietly.

When the two were seated at the Indian Queen, a small tavern on Chestnut Street at four o'clock, the usual dining hour, Washington quickly revealed what was on his mind.

For several days, he said, he was disturbed by strong hints from friends that he might be elected commander in chief of the army the delegates had openly talked about.

"After today's vote, someone might nominate me," Washington said.

"That would be wonderful!" was Pendleton's immediate response.

"Edmund," Washington said seriously, "I'm not qualified. I've never had any formal military training. Once, for a brief period, I commanded a small regiment. When I was with Braddock and Forbes, I commanded no one. I simply did their bidding and relayed their orders to the troops."

"You were much more important than that," Pendleton protested. "Besides, we have no one else. That's why everyone is leaning in your direction."

"But I don't want to take on such an enormous responsibility. I don't have the passion for arms and 'glory' that I had twenty years ago. I'm a farmer. And the past seventeen years have been the happiest of my life."

"And you expect to go home and raise crops while the rest of the country goes to war?" Pendleton asked sharply.

"Of course not! If called on, I'll serve with the Virginia militia. But I can't possibly take command of the whole army."

"Are you saying you'll refuse?"

Ignoring the question, Washington said, "Edmund, you've got to help put a stop to any campaign to elect me."

Pendleton looked into Washington's eyes and said firmly, "I won't ask anyone to vote against you. But before any vote, I could suggest that the Congress consider others."

A quiet "thank you" was all Washington could manage. He then dropped his head and toyed with his food, his mind far away.

Late the following day, John Adams again took the floor during another session of Congress. After addressing the chair, he said somberly, "We now face a difficult and delicate task. We must choose a man to command the new Continental Army we have now created. And while this may not be the proper moment to nominate that man, I can, without hesitation, tell you who I believe we should elect."

For a dramatic moment, Adams paused once again and looked around the room, trying to catch every eye.

"I have but one gentleman in mind for the important and critical post of commander in chief," he said. "He is a gentleman from Virginia. He is among us, and well known to all. He is a gentleman with considerable skill and experience as an officer; and a gentleman whose great talents and excellent universal character will command the approbation of all America. And a gentleman who will unite the cordial exertions of all the Colonies better than any other person in our union!"

Knowing who Adams had in mind, an embarrassed Washington slipped out of his chair and into an adjoining library. As he did so, he heard the clear sounds of approval. But the nomination did not come.

Hancock adjourned the meeting.

Realizing a vote would be coming, Washington remained in seclusion the next day, June 15. As a result, he did not hear how Edmund Pendleton, keeping his word, tried to turn the tide of sentiment toward another choice for Commander of the Army.

"What concerns me," Pendleton said to the assembled delegates, "is the effect the appointment of a Commander from outside of New England will have on the morale of the New England troops. Do they not already have a Commander? And one of their own?"

Ignoring this argument, Thomas Johnson of Maryland rose that sunny afternoon to say, "I hereby move that Congress elect George Washington as commander in chief of the Continental Army."

The motion was quickly seconded. No one else

was nominated. Washington was elected unanimously, a fact he learned at dinner when several smiling delegates greeted him with "Good evening, General Washington."

But would Washington accept the nomination? The answer came the next morning after John Hancock called for silence and made this brief announcement: "The President has the order of Congress to inform George Washington, Esquire, of the unanimous vote in choosing him to be General and commander in chief of the forces raised and to be raised in defense of American liberty. The Congress hopes the gentleman will accept."

Washington rose slowly from his seat to respond. He bowed stiffly to Hancock and then, looking neither to the right nor left, fumbled for something inside his tunic. A scrap of paper appeared. Washington, head down, began to read from it in a low, emotional voice: "Mr. President. Although I am truly sensible of the high honor done me in this appointment, I feel great distress from a consciousness that my abilities and military experience may not be equal to this extensive and important trust. However, as the Congress desires, I will enter upon the momentous duty, and exert every power I possess in their service for the support of our glorious cause. . . ."

After pausing to look at the delegates seated around him, he said in a louder, somewhat accusatory voice, "But lest some unlucky event should happen unfavorable to my reputation, I beg it may be remembered . . . that I, this day, declare with utmost sincerity, I do not think myself equal to the command I am honored with."

The delegates shifted uneasily in their seats.

Then, Washington made another startling statement. He would take no pay for his services. "Money," he said, "could never tempt me to accept this arduous employment at the expense of my domestic ease and happiness." And while he refused to "make any profit" from his command, he would keep an "exact count of my expenses." If they were paid, he said, "that is all I desire."

It was a wish Congress never fulfilled.

Washington immediately plunged into the huge task of organizing his command. His thoughts, however, constantly strayed to his home at Mount Vernon, Virginia.

"Martha has to be told," an inner voice kept reminding him. And for good reason; she was his wife, and they were deeply in love.

When they met years earlier at the Governor's Ball in Williamsburg, she was Mrs. Martha Dandridge Custis. She had married Daniel Custis at seventeen, and became widowed at twenty-five with two small children, Jacky and Patsy. In the spring of 1758, George and Martha became engaged after a brief courtship.

Washington joined the campaign of General

John Forbes that June. For an agonizing six months, he did not see the pretty, slightly plump widow he planned to marry. In November of that year, however, Fort Duquesne fell, bringing an end to the so-called French and Indian War.

After Washington's return to Virginia, he and Martha were reunited just in time for the Christmas season—a season that would remain special for them for the rest of their lives.

They were married on January 6, 1759. For almost seventeen years, he served in the House of Burgesses and devoted most of his attention to his family and Mount Vernon. But now, he thought sadly, he must leave her again and tell her about the escalating events in Philadelphia.

"My Dearest," he wrote with a heavy heart, "I am now set down to write you on a subject which fills me with inexpressible concern, and this concern is greatly aggravated and increased, when I reflect upon the uneasiness I know it will cause you. It has been determined in Congress that the whole army raised for the defence of the American cause shall be put under my care, and that it is necessary for me to proceed immediately to Boston.

"You may believe me, my dear, when I assure you in the most solemn manner that, so far from seeking this appointment, I have used every endeavor in my power to avoid it, not only from my unwillingness to part with you and the family, but from a consciousness of its being a trust too great for my capacity, and that I should enjoy more real happiness in one month with you at home than I have the most distant prospect of finding abroad if my stay were to be seven times seven years. But as it has been a kind of destiny that has thrown me upon this service, I shall hope that my undertaking is designed to answer some good purpose. . . . I shall feel no pain from the toil or the danger of the campaign; my unhappiness will flow from the uneasiness I know you will feel from being left alone. . . ."

As the letter drew to a close, Washington told Martha he was enclosing an important document drafted and witnessed by Edmund Pendleton. It was his will.

"As life is always uncertain," he carefully explained, "common prudence dictates to every man the necessity of settling his temporal concerns while it is in his power, and while the mind is calm and undisturbed. . . . The provision made for you in case of my death will, I hope, be agreeable."

Washington then added a postscript that surely must have softened the blow and perhaps brought a smile to Martha's lips and a tear to her eye: "I have bought two suits of the prettiest dress material on Chestnut Street today. And what a bargain it was! I hope it pleases you."

Only a handful of men in the Colonies had enough military experience to qualify as army officers, but at Washington's urging, the

Congress appointed four major generals, all of whom were to report directly to the commander.

The senior man, and second in command, was sickly Artemas Ward, already on the scene in Boston. Ward's experience was limited to one campaign in the French and Indian War.

The most experienced was Charles Lee, a skinny, foul-mouthed braggart and soldier-of-fortune who liked dogs and women, in that order. The forty-four-year-old Lee had joined the British army as a boy and had served with Braddock and Forbes during their campaigns against the French. It was then that he and Washington became acquainted.

Later, Lee became a major general in the Polish army in Europe and had fought against the Turks. When this part of his career ended, he moved to Virginia and often visited Washington.

Congress also gave top commands to Philip Schuyler of New York and Israel Putnam of Connecticut. Both, like Ward, had served on the frontier in the French and Indian War. But Washington needed more help of a professional nature. At his request, Congress gave Horatio Gates, another veteran of the British army, the highest post on the Headquarters Staff, adjutant general.

Gates, like Lee, had met Washington during the Braddock and Forbes campaigns. After reaching the rank of major general, however, he resigned and, at Washington's suggestion, moved to Virginia.

At the next level of command, Congress appointed eight brigadier generals. And while

Washington was authorized to appoint colonels, Congress decided that all other officers would be selected by the colonial assemblies whenever local militias were raised.

On June 22, as he was hurrying to leave Philadelphia, Washington received a vague report that the British had fought a battle with New England forces at Breed's and Bunker hills outside of Boston.

The report caused him to speed up his departure and pen another letter to his wife. "My Dearest," he wrote, "As I am within a few minutes of leaving this city, I could not think of departing from it without dropping you a line, especially as I do not know whether it may be in my power to write you again till I get to the camp at Boston. I go fully trusting in that Providence, which has been more bountiful to me than I deserve, and in full confidence of a happy meeting with you sometime in the Fall. . . ."

"Sometime in the Fall" was wishful thinking.

To save his horse for a long journey in warm weather, Washington liked to start before breakfast. He did so on June 23, leaving Philadelphia accompanied by Charles Lee and Philip Schuyler.

The three generals and several junior officers, including thirty-four-year-old Joseph Reed and thirty-one-year-old Thomas Mifflin, wore uniforms that were different in color, style, and material. Nevertheless, they were now all part of the same army.

In the commander's baggage were his orders, written by Richard Henry Lee, John Adams, and Edward Rutledge. Signed and approved by every member of Congress, the orders stated that the "Delegates Of The United Colonies" had empowered him to command "all the forces for the defense of American liberty and the repelling of invasion. . . .

"You are hereby vested with full power and authority to act as you think for the good and welfare of the service. . . ." In addition, Washington was told to conduct himself ". . . by the rules and discipline of war . . . and to punctually observe such orders and directions, from time to time, as you shall receive from this, or a future Congress of these United Colonies. . . ."

Lastly, the delegates stoutly declared they would "maintain and assist him, and adhere to him, the said George Washington, Esquire, with their lives and fortunes in the same cause."

These were not idle words. All realized that should colonial resistance be overcome in the days immediately ahead, they would be hunted down, arrested, and charged with treason, a crime that carried a severe penalty—death by hanging.

The fate of the Congress, the army, and the Colonies was now in the hands of one man: George Washington.

It was raining hard on a Sunday morning when Washington's horse, a chestnut gelding named Toby, shot his ears forward and turned his head toward a grove of trees to the left of the muddy road.

Looking in that direction, Washington saw four horsemen gathered beneath the dripping branches of a huge white oak.

As the riders came together, the leader of the group, a tall, good-looking man on a dappled gray mare called out, "Welcome! I'm Dr. Benjamin Church."

"Yes, Dr. Church," Washington responded with a warm smile. "I remember you. You're one of the reasons I'm here."

"You might say that," Dr. Church laughed. Church, the man who had delivered the plea to Congress to take over the army at Cambridge, then explained that he and his group would escort the general into Watertown, the temporary seat of the Massachusetts Provisional Congress.

"After a brief ceremony at the Congressional hall," he said, "we'll go with you to Cambridge, which is only about three or four miles away."

As they rode along, Washington learned that Church had just been appointed the army's director general of hospitals. He was also, Church said proudly, a member of the Boston delegation to the Provincial Congress, along with John Adams and

John Hancock, both of whom were still in Philadelphia. When Washington finally arrived in Cambridge, there was no one to greet him. In fact, the little town, home of Harvard College, seemed deserted.

He was not surprised, as he was supposed to have arrived a day earlier, on July 1. It didn't matter; he'd had enough of receptions on his ten-day journey. So, as soon as he found an officer and a fresh horse, he was off to inspect the Patriot lines.

From the top of several hills, with the aid of his telescope, he could see that Boston was on a peninsula. The city's only link to the mainland was a short, narrow strip of land south of the city called Boston Neck.

Directly north of the city was the Charlestown peninsula with Bunker Hill virtually in its center, now occupied and well fortified by the British.

Directly south of Boston lay Dorchester peninsula, an oddly shaped piece of land that measured about three miles between its widest east-west points and from a half mile to a mile from north to south. Significantly, the high ground—Nook's Hill and Dorchester Heights—faced three important objectives: Boston Harbor and the approach from the sea, Boston Neck, and the city itself. The entire Dorchester peninsula, however, was unoccupied by either army.

"There are advantages and disadvantages to our situation," Washington commented on the ride back to Cambridge. "We have the hills, they have the water and a navy. Obviously, we must increase our advantage and do what we can to minimize theirs."

But this was a tall order, as Washington soon found out.

O n returning to Cambridge, Washington called his generals and staff officers to a meeting at his temporary headquarters, the home of Samuel Langdon, president of Harvard College. Among those who attended was the rotund and effusive General Horatio Gates, who had just arrived.

Realizing that many of his officers had little or no formal military training, Washington explained that the meeting was to be a "council of war," a technique he learned from both the Indians he dealt with during the French and Indian War and the two British generals he had served.

He then carefully described how such councils were to be conducted. "I expect every man who has an opinion on the subjects being discussed to express that opinion," he said, "and to do so in a calm, concise, objective, and orderly manner.

"When options are developed, each officer will have the opportunity to vote on a course of action. I will have the final vote and make the final decision. When a decision has been reached, I expect every man—whether or not he agrees—to wholeheartedly support that decision. Any questions?"

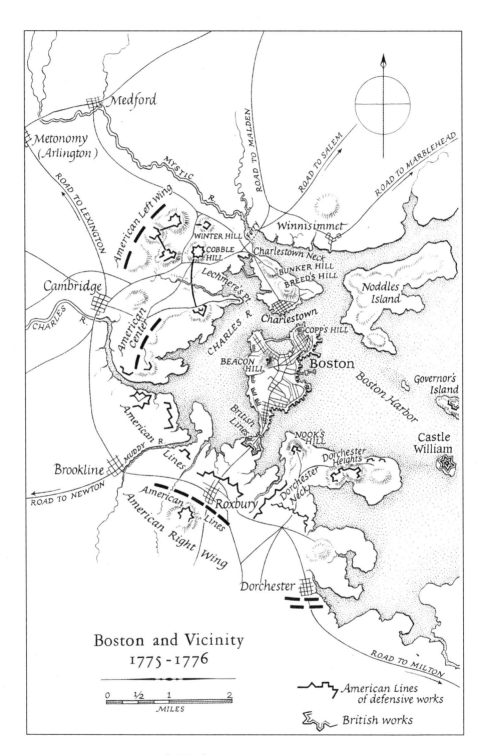

Boston and Vicinity
1775 - 1776

0   ½   1   2
MILES

⌐∿⌐∟   American Lines
       of defensive works

Σ⌐∿   British works

Medford

Metonomy
(Arlington)

ROAD TO LEXINGTON

ROAD TO MALDEN

ROAD TO SALEM

ROAD TO MARBLEHEAD

MYSTIC R.

American Left Wing

WINTER HILL

COBBLE HILL

Lechmere's Pt.

Winnisimmet

Charlestown Neck

BUNKER HILL

BREED'S HILL

Noddles Island

Cambridge

CHARLES R.

American Center

CHARLES R.

Charlestown

COPP'S HILL

BEACON HILL

Boston

Boston Harbor

Governor's Island

American R.

American Lines

British Lines

NOOK'S HILL

Castle William

Brookline

MUDDY R.

ROAD TO NEWTON

American Lines

Roxbury

Dorchester Neck

Dorchester Heights

American Right Wing

Dorchester

ROAD TO MILTON

[26]

Since there were none, Washington continued. "The purpose of this council is to assess our situation. There is much we need to digest before we can make any meaningful plans. First, what do we know about the British?"

General Artemas Ward answered immediately. "From those who have slipped through enemy lines and managed to cross to ours we know they have some eleven thousand regulars and marines in the city. The troops are well armed and equipped. Their force also includes five artillery companies. And in the waters around Boston there are some forty to fifty ships at any given time."

"In your opinion, will they attack?" the forty-seven-year-old General Gates asked.

"On any day, at any hour," Ward answered somberly.

There was a brief silence. Then Washington asked, "If that happens, how would you assess our situation?"

"Rotten," the former storekeeper answered sourly. "Most of the weapons we have belong to the men who carry them. None are new. Some are antiques. Many are of different makes. And some men have no weapons!"

Gates asked the next question. "What about food and shelter?"

"Shelter?" Ward snorted. "We have a few tents made of old sailcloth, and some of the men have built themselves huts made from scraps of wood.

The rest live in the open. As to food, we have plenty at the moment."

"And other supplies?" Washington asked.

"We have about three hundred short-range cannon of various types. We are extremely short of clothing and shoes. In fact, some of those who fought on Bunker and Breed's hills are practically naked. In six weeks, we'll need warm clothing and blankets."

Although fearful of the answer, Washington asked another question. "What about powder?"

"Very low," Ward said sadly.

"How low?"

"Thirty-six barrels."

"Thirty-six barrels?" Lee asked in disbelief. "That's all?"

"That's all," Ward answered. "And, by my calculation, it comes out to about nine rounds per man. Furthermore, by the end of the year we'll need a new army."

Lee hit the council table so hard with the flat of his right hand that he woke up the pair of hound dogs slumbering at his feet.

"This could be the shortest damned war in military history!" he roared.

Despite the candid comments of General Ward, the council of war failed to expose all of the weaknesses of the new, ragtag Continental Army, which was made up of mostly shopkeepers and farmers, but also included a smattering of blacks, Indians, and children. But it didn't matter. Washington easily recognized most of the problems as he went through the camps and front lines. What he saw, heard, and sensed led to these conclusions:

- Fortifications in general were so poorly constructed and so badly placed that they were virtually worthless.
- The chain of command, vital to the success of any army, was practically nonexistent.
- It was almost impossible to know who was in command of many units because officers and privates wore their own clothes.
- Troops from the different colonies were often so independent that they were prone to ignore a central command.
- Many of the officers in the lower ranks were political appointees without military experience, and most didn't know what was expected of them.
- Thievery, insubordination, desertion, and even cowardice among officers and privates made it clear the army lacked a code of conduct and a method of enforcing discipline.
- There were no precautions against a surprise attack, such as an early warning system, or an established intelligence network.

After studying and weighing these facts Washington saw that he had but two choices: to keep the British troops, now under command of General William Howe, bottled up in Boston until the king's ministers came to their senses; and to organize, train, supply, and increase the size of his army as quickly as possible.

But would the British remain dormant long enough to enable him to reach these goals? To Washington, that seemed highly unlikely.

"On any day, at any hour." Haunted by General Ward's words, Washington immediately tackled the huge task of preparing the army for the worst that could happen—an immediate all-out clash with the enemy.

He began by splitting the army into three "grand divisions," each with two brigades. The division on the right wing was situated at Roxbury and faced British positions on Boston Neck. General Ward was in command with two brigades under John Thomas and Joseph Spencer.

General Lee was put in command of the division on the left, facing Bunker Hill and the rest of the Charlestown peninsula. One brigade was headed by John Sullivan of New Hampshire. The other brigadier under Lee was thirty-three-year-old Nathanael Greene of Rhode Island, a rugged, able officer whose stiff right knee gave him a perpetual, unsoldierly limp.

Israel Putnam was in command of the center, facing Boston's Beacon Hill across the Charles River with brigades to be assigned later.

In the first sentence of his first "General Orders," Washington attempted to get a firm grip on the critical matter of supplies. He asked that the "proper officers" forward to Headquarters an exact count of ". . . all the provisions, stores, Powder, Lead, working tools of all kinds, Tents, Camp Kettles and all other stores under their respective care." He also asked the commanding officer of each regiment to forward a count of the number of blankets needed, so each man would have ". . . one at least."

Washington said that since Congress had taken militia from different colonies into its "service and pay," they were now the troops of "The United Provinces of North America. It is hoped that all distinctions of colonies will be laid aside," he added, "so that one and the same spirit may animate the whole, and the only contest be, who shall render, on this great and trying occasion, the most essential service to the great and common cause in which we are all engaged. . . ."

In the same orders, he said that army rules and regulations forbid the use of profanity and "drunkenness."

Washington also:

- urged the men to attend "divine service" when not on duty.
- asked officers ". . . to visit [their men] often in their quarters" and to ". . . inculcate upon them the necessity of cleanliness, as essential to their health and service."
- ordered regimental commanders to see to it that not more than two men of a company be absent on furlough at the same time.
- forbade the firing of cannon or small arms from any of the lines except on orders.
- ordered that all prisoners, deserters, and civilians coming out of Boston were to be brought to Headquarters for questioning.

Washington then called on his men to observe "exact discipline and due subordination" and reminded them that ". . . failure in these most essential points must necessarily produce extreme hazard, disorder and confusion; and end in shameful disappointment and disgrace."

With these remarkable "Orders," dated July 4, 1775, Washington established the foundation for today's United States Army.

At the time, there was much more to be done.

Without letup, a steady stream of "Orders" continued to pour out of Washington's Headquarters, triggering a host of activities.

Starting at 4:00 A.M. each day, for example, rotating groups of troops were soon on the hills with picks, shovels, and axes building redoubts and other defenses. Those men not in a work detail were drilled and trained or performed other duties.

Every night, whale boats manned by John Glover's Marblehead regiment patrolled the waters near every possible landing site. On shore, saddled horses were tied to trees, ready to be ridden inland at a gallop to warn of a possible invasion.

An intelligence network was also established utilizing residents of Boston. A signaling system to warn of troop movements included flashing lights from church steeples at night, and a meaningful series of explosions during daylight. Other citizens helped by circulating propaganda, such as exaggerated reports about Washington's supply of powder and recruits.

In addition, Washington hired a full-time spy. His instructions to the spy were brief: "Go into the town, learn all you can and communicate with me and no one else."

To harass and, with luck, capture British supply boats moving in or out of Boston, Washington acquired a small, swift "navy" by hiring scores of New England captains and arming their vessels. Their reward was one-third the value of any cargo confiscated.

Washington also concentrated on improving the quality of his officers, regardless of rank. And to distinguish differences in rank, ribbons were soon being worn on the breast of every officer; light blue for Washington, pink for brigadiers, purple for major generals, and green for staff officers. Others wore different cockades in their hats or a strip of colored cloth on the right shoulder.

While all this was going on, Washington bombarded Congress and the Provincial governments with twin pleas: More troops! More powder!

While Congress did its best to comply, it still hoped for peace. It petitioned King George to end aggression, repeal the Coercive Acts, and bring about "a happy and permanent reconciliation."

The king said that the Colonies were in "open rebellion" and vowed "to suppress such rebellion and bring the traitors to justice."

War—all-out war—was now inevitable.

When the Patriots seized Fort Ticonderoga in May 1775, the way was opened for an invasion of British-held Canada. But Congress held back. Late in June, however, Congress changed its mind.

As a result, Philip Schuyler, commander of the army's Northern Department, headquartered at Albany, New York, was ordered to make preparations for a Canadian campaign.

As the summer months went by, Washington came up with a daring plan to break the British hold on Canada by capturing their garrisons at Montreal and Quebec.

The plan had two objectives: (1) Eliminate the possibility that the British could make a drive south to the Hudson River and meet a force coming north from New York City—a move that would split the New England colonies away from the rest; and (2) Pave the way for the Americans to establish a fourteenth colony in a territory once held by the French and still occupied by French citizens.

Schuyler, one of the generals who had left Philadelphia with the newly appointed commander in chief earlier in the year, reluctantly agreed to the plan and eventually named General Richard Montgomery as the leader of the troops that would attack Montreal.

For the attack on Quebec, Washington handpicked troops from his own army. To lead this force, Washington selected a man he had just met, a thirty-four-year-old colonel of rugged medium build who had a dark face, prominent nose, and unusually pale-blue eyes.

Washington told his council he had interviewed the man extensively. "He favors an attack on Quebec," he said. "And he's a proven leader and fighter."

The colonel's name was Benedict Arnold. Despite protests by Gates, Arnold was approved.

One evening in early September, Brigadier General Nathanael Greene, accompanied by a stranger in civilian clothes, was granted a private audience with Washington at Headquarters.

The civilian was Godfrey Wainwood, a baker who lived in Newport, Rhode Island. Greene explained that Wainwood had a letter for Washington, one that could be very important.

Washington was taken aback. "A letter?" he asked Wainwood. "You came all the way from Newport to deliver a letter?"

"Y-yes sir," the nervous Wainwood gulped as he jabbed a letter in Washington's direction.

After one glance at the contents, a puzzled Washington said, "It's in code!"

"So it is, sir," Greene responded calmly. "And addressed to a 'Major Cane in Boston of His Majesty's Service.'"

Turning to Wainwood, Washington asked sharply, "Who gave you this letter?"

"A woman named, uh, Yvonne," was the answer.

"What's her last name?"

"I don't know."

"But you're acquainted with her?"

"I, uh, knew her long ago. But only briefly, sir. I swear!"

"Do you know who wrote the letter?"

"No sir. But Yvonne sent it to me and asked me to deliver it to James Wallace. He's the captain of

Long before this portrait of Brigadier General Nathanael Greene was painted, General Washington called on him to apprehend America's first traitor.

H.M.S. *Rose*, now in Newport. And she said that if I couldn't get it to him, I should try to reach Charles Dudley or George Rome."

"Who are they?"

"Dudley is the Crown's tax collector in Newport, and Rome is a known Tory," Greene answered.

Washington nodded grimly, then turned to Wainwood again.

"This Yvonne. Do you know where she lives?"

"She said she lives here."

"Cambridge?" Washington asked, clearly alarmed. "Then the author of this letter, an obvious spy, may also be in Cambridge!"

Washington turned to Greene. "Find Yvonne and bring her in," he said. "But do it quietly."

It was close to midnight when Brigadier General Greene brought a brown-haired, brown-eyed woman to Headquarters. She had been pretty once, Washington observed, but now her features were coarse and drawn. And she was obviously pregnant.

It also became known that she was a prostitute who had known Wainwood, the baker, for a brief period before hostilities erupted with England.

Yvonne was stubbornly evasive about the identity of whoever wrote the coded letter. Finally, after hours of questioning, she admitted she was the mistress of the author.

"And he's the father of the child you are expecting?" Washington asked.

Yvonne nodded.

"What's his name?"

Sobbing, Yvonne remained silent.

"His name, Yvonne," Washington prodded. "Give me his name."

"Dr. . . . . Church," Yvonne wailed, a handkerchief pressed against her eyes.

"Dr. Church?" Washington gasped. "Dr. Benjamin Church?"

Convulsed in sobs, Yvonne could only nod.

Washington acted swiftly. Two cryptographers were routed out of bed and asked to independently decipher the letter. When Washington saw the results, he shot a grim order to his aides:

"Bring Dr. Church to Headquarters immediately."

Dr. Church seemed calm enough when Washington confronted him about the letter.

"Yes," he said, "I wrote it. I was sending it to my brother, Fleming Church, in Boston."

"Tell me, Dr. Church," Washington said pleasantly, "why did you find it necessary to use a private emissary to send a letter to your brother through Newport and on to the military? Couldn't you have sent it by ordinary means?"

"I wanted to be sure my brother got the letter," Dr. Church answered. "And I put it in code because there were some private matters I needed to convey to him."

"Private matters?" Washington asked.

"Yes, nothing criminal."

"Nothing criminal, you say?"

"Of course not!" Church blustered.

Washington suddenly thrust a decoded copy of the letter in front of Church's nose. "You have been corresponding regularly with the British top command," he barked. "You, a trusted member of the Provincial Congress. A friend and colleague of John Adams and John Hancock. A man who has access to a wealth of military secrets. In this letter alone, you describe the strength and equipment of colonial forces. You tell them of our plans to commission privateers. You tell them we intend to march on Canada.

"And then you say, 'This advice is the result of our affection for my King and to the Realm. Remember I never deceived you; every article here sent you is sacredly true. Make use of every precaution or I perish.'"

Washington stood and looked at Church with cold contempt.

"Dr. Church," he said, his voice quivering with anger, "you are a traitor. And you will hang!"

Church did not hang. The Army Code adopted by Congress provided no punishment for traitorous acts by civilians. Washington had no choice but to turn Church over to the Provincial Congress. He was jailed but subsequently given permission to leave the country for the West Indies. A storm sank his ship. All aboard perished.

And while this was Washington's first encounter with a traitor, it would not be his last.

Winter came quickly to Massachusetts in 1775. By early November the ground was frozen, snow had fallen several times, and the temperature, pushed down by howling winds from the northwest, remained numbingly low.

This hampered efforts to build shelters for the troops, already poorly clad and without enough blankets. As a result, the shivering men complained bitterly about living conditions.

With the enlistments of 3,700 Connecticut soldiers to expire as early as December 1 and others to follow, Washington clearly faced a serious crisis. At a council of war he said, "With so many spies in and around Cambridge, the enemy will quickly learn of our weakened condition and they may take the opportunity to attack. Perhaps we should take the initiative now."

The council voted to do nothing "at this time."

In Washington's mind, however, a solution to the army's dilemma began to take shape.

On November 16, Washington called twenty-five-year-old Captain Henry Knox to Headquarters. Knox, he was told, once owned the

London Book Shop in Boston and had an odd hobby: the study of guns and fortifications.

Other facts he gleaned from a briefing were that Knox lost the third and fourth fingers of his left hand when his fowling piece exploded while hunting and that he was present at the so-called "Boston Massacre" and tried to prevent the shooting. Having joined the Massachusetts militia at eighteen, he was in the battle for Bunker Hill and had fought well. Just as tall as Washington, he was at least fifty pounds heavier.

"Captain," Washington said, "I have a mission for you that is difficult and may fail. Nevertheless, I want you to do your best to carry it through."

"Yes, sir," was all a puzzled Knox could say.

"General Schuyler and Colonel Arnold both told me there are several long-range cannon at Fort Ticonderoga," Washington said, watching Knox carefully.

"So I've heard," Knox said.

"And, as you probably know, Ti is almost three hundred miles from here, with forests, mountains, lakes, and rivers in between."

"Yes, sir," Knox said, still a bit bewildered.

Washington waited a moment, then said bluntly, "Do you think you can get the guns and bring them here?"

Knox's round face suddenly glowed. "I'd like to try, sir!" he said.

"Good," Washington said with a smile and a clap of his hand on Knox's beefy shoulder.

Washington didn't tell Knox or anyone else about his plans. That had to wait until Knox completed his mission—if he could.

Two-thirds of the Connecticut troops refused to re-enlist toward the end of November and later marched home, but there were bright spots in the midst of this and other depressing news that engulfed Washington in the winter of 1775.

The holds of a captured British brig named *Nancy* yielded two thousand stand of small arms, hundreds of flints, tons of musket shot, and a thirteen-inch mortar.

For Washington, however, a second bit of news was even more exciting and welcome: Martha Washington, ignoring warnings that she could be captured and exchanged for the commander in chief, would soon be on her way to Cambridge.

Leaving Virginia for the first time in her life, she did not make the three-week journey to far-off Boston alone or without fanfare. With her in the family carriage was her son, Jacky; her pregnant daughter-in-law, Nelly; Mrs. Horatio Gates, and a maid. At virtually every large town she was met by an escort and greeted as "Lady Washington."

When she finally reached Headquarters, she stepped groggily out of the carriage into deep snow and looked around in bewilderment. Suddenly, a pair of long arms was wrapped around her from behind. "Welcome to Cambridge," her husband said.

Headquarters was now established in a large, beautiful home belonging to a departed Tory. At Christmastime, with Washington's encouragement, Martha decorated the house with tinsel and garlands.

And on the hills that could be seen in Boston, he ordered his men to build huge bonfires after dark, hoping that word would reach the city that he was unconcerned about an attack and that the Americans were warm, well-fed, and enjoying the Christmas holiday.

On the final day of the year, his troops were reduced to some 11,000, the army's weakest point. Still, if the British knew this, they didn't attack.

Bad news, however, poured in from every quarter during the first days of 1776. Norfolk had been razed by Virginia's Royal Governor, Lord Dunmore. King George announced he was adding mercenaries from Russia and Germany to his own military might. His objective, he said, was to crush a rebellion "aimed at establishing an independent empire," an idea that never had occurred to most Americans. Furthermore, four more regiments he had sent to Boston had just arrived.

The two-pronged attempt to invade Canada had been in trouble from the beginning. Richard Montgomery's forces, ravaged by sickness and short of supplies, was held up for two months at the British-held fort at St. John's.

Benedict Arnold had fared as badly. Heavy rains and winter weather ruined the bulk of his supplies, and the trip through the wildest country imaginable took twice the time he had calculated.

After capturing Montreal, Montgomery had gone to Quebec to join Arnold. In an assault on that stronghold, Montgomery was killed and Arnold wounded. Arnold, with his force reduced to six hundred men, held on outside the city during the bitter winter months. Despite a valiant attempt to continue the campaign, British reinforcements arrived by ship in the spring and eventually forced the battered Americans to withdraw, again leaving the Colonies vulnerable to a thrust from Canada.

Ironically, on the day a copy of the king's speech reached Boston, Washington had raised a new flag at Headquarters. It contained thirteen red and white stripes, but had the Union Jack, the flag of Britain, in the canton (the upper left-hand corner). A Boston civilian remarked to Washington, "Everyone in the city thought your new flag meant you were ready to surrender."

"Not yet," was Washington's grim response.

A few weeks later, as replacements began to pour into the camps, it grew so cold that much of the water around Boston became a thick sheet of ice. After riding to the shoreline below Cambridge, Washington dismounted, walked out on the ice, and jumped up and down. Less than an hour later, he told another council, "We can't wait any longer. We've got to cross to Boston!"

"On the ice?" General Greene asked.

"On the ice," Washington said firmly.

Too risky and premature was the vote. A few days later, however, a courier brought news that caused Washington's heart to leap with joy: Henry Knox had returned!

Knox didn't know it, but during his absence from Cambridge, he had been promoted from captain to colonel. It was a well-deserved promotion, for he had performed a herculean feat.

Knox had arrived in Ticonderoga on December 5. In less than a month, he selected the guns he wanted, had forty-two large sledges built, and located sixty-eight yoke of oxen to pull them. In all, he transported fifty-two cannon, nine large mortars, and five cohorns. Three of the thirteen-inch siege guns, including one dubbed "Old Sow," weighed a ton each. In addition to the guns, which totaled almost 20,000 pounds, the convoy carried 2,300 pounds of lead and a barrel of flints.

During a harrowing return to camp, Knox faced many difficult and often hazardous obstacles. Still, he made the three hundred-mile return trip with remarkable speed.

Major General Henry Knox, a hero in the successful siege of Boston, was commander of artillery throughout the war and later became secretary of war under President Washington.

"Well done, Henry!" exulted Washington when he learned the guns were parked in Framingham, some twenty miles from Cambridge.

Since he didn't have the power or means to cross to Boston by water and drive the British from the city, Washington had devised a scheme that had but one objective: Lure the British into an attack. Then smash them!

On February 27, Washington's General Orders sent a wave of excitement and anticipation through the ranks.

"As the season is now fast approaching when every man must expect to be drawn into the field of action," Washington told his troops, "it is highly necessary that he should prepare his mind as well as everything necessary for it. It is a noble cause we are engaged in; it is the cause of virtue and mankind. Every temporal advantage and comfort to us and our posterity depends upon the vigor of our exertions. In short, freedom or slavery must be the result of our conduct."

He then warned that the men must conduct themselves as soldiers. "If any man in action shall presume to skulk, hide himself, or retreat from the enemy, without the orders of his commanding officer, he will be instantly shot down, as an example of cowardice!"

After dark on March 2, Patriot guns, their shots spaced far apart to save powder, opened up on the left. The British responded vigorously, but to little effect.

Two nights later, as cannons again began to roar, some three thousand men quietly climbed to the crests of Dorchester Heights. With them went a train of the three hundred oxcarts loaded with prefabricated fortifications and the long-range Ticonderoga guns, including "Old Sow." At 3 A.M., with surprising precision and very little noise, a fatigue party of another three thousand replaced the first wave of workers.

The oxcarts completed two more trips. When dawn broke, the Patriots promptly put down their tools, picked up their guns, and moved to their assigned places.

They were ready.

After a bright morning sun burned away the morning fog, British gunners on Boston Neck discovered to their utter amazement that the hills of Dorchester Heights were now occupied by several thousand Americans standing quietly next to their guns and grinning down at them.

They promptly opened fire with their batteries. It was no use. The redcoats couldn't elevate their guns enough to hit their jeering targets!

Looking through his glass at Boston, Washington could see little activity. But he was not deceived. "High tide is at noon," he told his officers. "That's when they'll come. If they don't come then, they will on the next flood."

Totally unprepared for Washington's audacious maneuver, the British missed the first tide. Recovering quickly, troops and artillery were rushed aboard ships that were soon at anchor at Castle William, an island in the ship channel just east of Dorchester Heights.

As Washington hoped, the enemy planned to come ashore on the next tide and storm the newly discovered American fortifications. That afternoon, however, gale winds and a fierce rainstorm struck the Boston area. British plans were abandoned.

On the afternoon of March 8, a white flag of truce suddenly appeared at the front of the British lines on Boston Neck. A British officer and three civilians came forward and handed an American officer a letter for General Washington from the city's Selectmen.

When Washington broke the seal, he gasped in surprise, then read the first line aloud: "As His Excellency General Howe is determined to leave the town with the troops under his command . . ."

"He's leaving?" an incredulous aide broke in.

"So it seems," Washington answered. "And, according to this, Howe promises not to burn the town if we don't fire on his ships."

After a stalemate of some eight months, a clear victory was in sight. Still, thought Washington, it could be a trick.

For eight days, Washington patiently watched the British load their ships with men and supplies. He could wait no longer. During the night of March 16, the Americans began operations on Nook's Hill just as they had weeks earlier on Dorchester Heights.

By morning, the American gun emplacements sent a clear signal to the British: Leave immediately or risk the loss of every ship in the harbor and every soldier in the town.

Boston wharves were soon filled with redcoats boarding the small boats that would take them to their ships. And by the end of the day, with a favorable wind, British sails filled the horizon to the east and soon disappeared.

That same day, some 1,500 Americans crossed to Boston from several points to secure the town. With little doubt, Boston was a major victory for the Continental Army.

But Washington knew—as every officer knew—that somewhere his small and still inexperienced Continental Army must again contend with British might. And the next engagement would not be as bloodless as Boston.

When the enemy left Boston, Washington asked himself this question: What would I do if I were General Howe?

The answer: Get control of the Hudson River, starting with New York City and the harbor at the mouth of the river.

With New York as a base of operations, the British, with their huge fleet, could invade the coastal harbors and rivers of virtually every colony. By driving south from Canada and up the Hudson from New York, they could split the four New England colonies away from the rest and seriously disrupt trade and communications.

New York, then, became Washington's immediate objective. He realized, of course, that without additional troops it would be almost impossible to hold the city for long against a foe with a large fleet. But there was no alternative. "For the British, New York is the key to conquering America," he told his officers.

On his arrival in New York on April 13, Washington established Headquarters near the tip of Manhattan in a three-story attached building on Pearl Street. A mile north, he found a house for himself and Martha, who arrived from Cambridge eleven days later with Jacky and Nelly.

Headquarters was not far from a four-thousand-pound gilded lead statue that irritated Washington and local Patriots, but was revered by New York's Tories; it was the figure of King George III dressed as a Roman emperor astride a magnificent horse.

Toward the end of Washington's first month in the city, there was bad news pouring in from several directions. The worst included details of the retreat from Canada.

On May 6, he learned, five British vessels reached Quebec with reinforcements for Sir Guy Carleton. The British commander promptly attacked weakened American positions outside the city with a battery of field artillery and a thousand men.

"Our forces were so dispersed that not more than two hundred could be collected at Headquarters," read a dispatch that Washington received two weeks later. "In this situation, a retreat was inevitable, and made in the utmost precipitation and confusion, with the loss of our cannon, provisions, five hundred stands of small arms and a bateau load of powder. Two hundred men too ill to move were left to the mercy of the enemy."

Washington also heard from Congress that General William Howe's brother, Admiral Richard Howe, had left England with a large fleet loaded with British redcoats and German mercenaries.

At about this time, several warships and transports were sighted off Cape Fear, North Carolina, confirming the belief that the British planned to attack Charleston, South Carolina. This word came in a letter from Charles Lee, who, to the dismay of local residents, occupied the ornate Governor's Palace in Williamsburg, Virginia, with his hound dogs and was known to frequently party in the revered ballroom with several unsavory lady friends.

Lee, put in command of the Southern Department by Congress, said he was on his way to Charleston to set up defenses and train the local militia. He closed his letter with: "My love to Mrs. Washington, Mrs. Gates and her bad half. . . . Adieu, my dear General."

"Such impertinence!" Martha snorted when Washington read the last lines to her. Washington laughed, but soon changed the subject.

"Martha," he said, kindly but firmly, "I'm taking you to Philadelphia to be inoculated against smallpox. If you refuse again, you will have to go home."

It was an on-and-off-again argument that had begun in Boston. But smallpox, a killer disease, was now running wild through the army. The only defense against it was inoculation. The procedure was dangerous, however, because it involved infecting a healthy person with a light dose of the disease.

After more argument, Martha reluctantly agreed to the treatment.

Late in May, while Martha was in a Philadelphia hospital being treated by the army's top physician, Washington met frequently with Congress just a short distance away.

He also dined often with the Virginia delegation. On one such occasion, he learned that the Virginians were about to introduce a resolution declaring that the colonies ought to be "free and independent states," a development that delighted Washington.

In a letter to his brother John Augustine, he said, "I am very glad to find that the Virginia Convention have passed so noble a vote, and with such unanimity. Things have come to that pass now as to convince us that we have nothing more to expect from the justice of Great Britain. . . ."

When introduced by Richard Henry Lee, however, the resolution caused an uproar. Many argued that the Colonies could not survive as independent states.

"Suicide!" one delegate shouted.

"It's like a child being thrown violently out of his father's house," another cried.

John Adams had the opposite view, calling out repeatedly, "A union and a confederation of thirteen states, independent of Parliament, of Ministers and a King!"

After considerable debate, the Virginia resolution was tabled for three weeks to give several of the colonies time to consult their respective assemblies. It would then be brought up for a vote.

Washington returned to New York on June 6 after a fast two-day ride. By then, Martha had fully recovered from the inoculation, but remained in Philadelphia as a guest of John Hancock and his new bride, Dolly, to await developments.

A few days later, Washington sent this depressing news to Congress: "In Canada the situation of our affairs is truly alarming. . . . General [William] Thompson has met with a repulse at Three Rivers, and is now a Prisoner in the hands of General John Burgoyne, who has arrived with considerable Army. . . . It is greatly to be feared . . . that our shattered, divided and broken Army have been obliged to abandon the Country and retreat to avoid a greater calamity, that of being cut off or becoming prisoners. . . ." He also noted that General Arnold had been forced to give up Montreal and General John Thomas had since died of smallpox. Canada, it became clear, was lost.

The same day, however, this was overshadowed when three very excited members of the New York Committee of Safety—John Jay, Gouverneur Morris, and Philip Livingston—rushed into Washington's office on Pearl Street.

"Excellency, we have uncovered a plot against the army!" Jay blurted out without preliminaries.

"With so many Tories in this town, I'm not surprised," Washington said calmly, his mind still on events in Canada.

The three committee members exchanged looks. Then Livingston said in a low, halting voice, "But, sir, you don't understand. You may be the main target."

"And," Morris quickly joined in, "the Headquarters Guard has been implicated!"

Washington was stunned. The Headquarters Guard? It couldn't be true! But suppose—?

"Bring me the evidence," he said grimly.

Washington, always looking for ways to instill discipline and pride in his army, had created the Headquarters Guard just before he left Cambridge earlier that spring.

The Guard, according to the order issued at the time, was to consist of forty volunteers; "handsome and well made men" who were "neat and spruce" and measured between five feet eight inches and five feet ten inches in height.

When finally selected, the Guard, which included two drummers, two fifers, and a black soldier named Tobias Gilmore, was put under the command of a New Englander, Captain Caleb Gibbs.

In addition to ceremonial duties, the Guard was charged with the safety of the commander in chief, the Headquarters staff, and Headquarters facilities.

"For the Guard to be compromised by the enemy is shocking, to say the least," Washington told General Greene, who was called in to help with the investigation. "I want to get to the bottom of this immediately." By the end of the day, the investigators uncovered the story.

Thomas Hickey and Michael Lynch, members of the Headquarters Guard, had been arrested for passing counterfeit money. While in jail, they boasted that they were members of the King's Militia, a group of seven hundred American soldiers being paid by the British. They bragged that with the arrival of the British fleet and the landing of troops—which could happen almost any day—the turncoats would cut down King's Bridge at the north end of Manhattan Island, seize the artillery, and turn it on their fellow Americans.

If anything went wrong, William Greene, a drummer and one of four other Guard members named, was to sneak up on an unsuspecting Washington at Headquarters and stab him to death.

According to one witness, a written list of the men who agreed to the plot had been sent aboard the *Asia,* a British man-of-war anchored in the outer harbor. The list, it was said, had been signed by Hickey.

The first person implicated in the plot, however, was the mayor of New York, David Matthews. Witnesses said he had gone aboard the *Duchess of Gordon* and was given a bundle of cash by the governor of New York, William Tryon, to pass on to Hickey and other conspirators.

On Washington's orders, issued at one o'clock the next morning, General Greene promptly boarded a boat with two of his men, crossed to Brooklyn, marched to Matthews's home, routed the suspect out of bed, seized his papers, and put him under arrest.

Like the traitor Dr. Benjamin Church, Mayor Matthews was turned over to local authorities. Charged with " . . . dangerous designs and treasonable conspiracies against the rights and liberties of the United Colonies of America," he was promptly found guilty and jailed.

One by one, all of those in the army known to have been involved in the conspiracy were court-martialed. Most confessed and threw themselves on the mercy of the court. Only Thomas Hickey showed no remorse.

The evidence against Hickey was conclusive. His only defense was to tell a few weak lies, and make a statement that his involvement with prostitutes led to his downfall. The verdict, rendered quickly, was unanimous: "Guilty as charged." He was sentenced to death by hanging.

Washington approved the decision immediately. In doing so, he told his staff, "We must make an example of Hickey. We can't have such a thing happen again."

He ordered a scaffold and a gallows built in the large, open square dominated by the statue of King George. As the work went on, word spread quickly.

By the time the noose was put around Hickey's neck, 20,000 people—virtually the entire population of New York—crowded the area to watch the macabre event.

When it was over, Washington had a message read to each brigade and posted about the city: "The unhappy fate of Thomas Hickey, executed this day for mutiny, sedition, and treachery, the General hopes will be a warning to every soldier in the Army to avoid those crimes and all others, so disgraceful to the character of a soldier and pernicious to his country, whose pay he receives and bread he eats.

"And in order to avoid those crimes, the most certain method is to keep out of the temptation of them, and particularly to avoid lewd women, who, by the dying confession of this poor criminal, first led him into practices which ended in an untimely and ignominious death."

"The flags are up!"

This message, rushed to Washington early on the morning of June 29, meant only one thing: The British fleet had finally arrived.

The flags were on a trio of staffs planted atop a high hill on Staten Island. Three red flags on the middle staff, one above the other, meant the enemy was headed to New York; two, to Amboy, New Jersey.

"Destination?" Washington barked when he got the word.

On June 29, 1775, part of a British fleet of 130 warships began arriving in New York Harbor.

"New York, sir," came the reply.

"How many ships?"

"So far, forty-five."

But the ships kept coming. Soon, 130 were anchored off Sandy Hook, each of them bulging with troops, supplies, and weapons.

After sending General Greene to Long Island with five thousand troops, Washington rushed a message to each New England colony that read: "Lose not a moment in sending forward the militia of your province as the enemy will undoubtedly attack us in our weakened state as soon as their forces are organized."

He also alerted Congress to the situation, saying, "I am hopeful before the British are prepared to attack that I shall get some reenforcements, but be that as it may, I shall attempt to make the best disposition I can for our troops, in order to give them a proper reception, and to prevent the ruin and destruction they are meditating against us."

As he watched the maneuvering of British ships around Long Island and Staten Island, Washington was troubled by several reports received from the Northern Department.

The Americans had retreated to Crown Point, just north of Ticonderoga, and Generals Schuyler and Gates were fighting over who was in command. Congress had put Gates in charge of the army in Canada. But that army was no longer in Canada. It was in New York, where Schuyler insisted that only he could command.

Enraged by Gates's appointment, Brigadier John Sullivan added to the furor by threatening to resign. Schuyler soothed his ruffled feathers and sent him to Washington, who was glad to have him.

Leaving it to Congress to settle the Gates–Schuyler squabble, Washington concentrated on his own problems.

"Where will they strike and when?" he constantly asked. No one had an answer. But a British army deserter, brought to Headquarters late one night, gave Washington and his staff a clue.

"They'll do nothing until the Admiral arrives in a week or two," the deserter said.

And so, with the stage set, the leading character, Admiral Viscount Richard Howe, General William Howe's brother, was about to come out of the wings. When he did, this much was clear: New York would not be like Boston, a standoff that ended with very little loss of life on either side. New York would be the scene of Washington's first major battle.

On July 9, Washington suddenly realized something else: New York might determine the fate of America. For that was the day two excited riders on hot horses brought word from John Hancock about an act of Congress that had taken place five days earlier.

The only person in Headquarters on that hot, muggy evening of July 9 was the commander in chief. Unseen, he sat close to an open window facing Pearl Street, ears straining to catch any sound that might be carried his way on a faint southwesterly breeze.

His order, written earlier that day, was already in the hands of his top command. It read: "The

Continental Congress, impelled by the dictates of duty, policy, and necessity, having been pleased to dissolve the Connection which subsisted between this Country, and Great Britain, and to declare the United Colonies of North America, free and independent States: The several brigades are to be drawn up this evening on their respective Parades, at Six O'Clock, when the declaration of Congress, showing the grounds and reasons of this measure, is to be read with an audible voice.

"The General hopes this important Event will serve as a fresh incentive to every officer, and soldier, to act with Fidelity and Courage, as knowing that now the peace and safety of his Country depends under God solely on the success of our arms: And that he is now in the service of a State, possessed of sufficient power to reward his merit, and advance him to the Honors of a free Country."

At precisely six o'clock the voices of several men—some deep, some high-pitched, some with a drawl or twang—started a reading that began: "When in the course of human events . . ."

When the voices neared the end, Washington grew tense, for now he would learn the answer to a question that had haunted him all day: Would the troops stay and fight a battle against overwhelming odds, or would they simply go home?

". . . And for the support of this Declaration, with a firm reliance on the protection of Divine Providence, we mutually pledge to each other our Lives, our Fortunes and our sacred honor."

For the briefest moment, there was silence. Then a crescendo of cheers! Musket shots! And, unaccountably, the sound of running feet!

Alarmed, Washington rushed to the door. "Halt! Halt!" he shouted in dismay.

It was no use. Scores of soldiers and civilians were stampeding toward the statue of King George and his horse. In no time, several men had fastened ropes around the statue. After several shouts of "heave-ho!" the horse and rider crashed to the ground.

With a "heave ho!," Patriot soldiers pulled down a statue of King George in New York after they heard a reading of the Declaration of Independence. Although the incident angered Washington, it showed that his men meant to fight.

While Washington was angered by the disorderly behavior of his men, he was heartened by their display of loyalty. He was also pleased with something else: When melted down, the King's deposed statue would provide four thousand pounds of lead that could be shaped into bullets!

Some people in the New York area were unhappy about the Declaration of Independence. Others didn't seem to understand the implications of the signing.

The day after the public reading in the city, for example, British troops went ashore on Staten Island just a few miles away and, to Washington's chagrin, were given a warm welcome by scores of residents, most of them Tories.

The same day, several companies of riflemen calmly packed up and went home, their enlistments ended. And while five hundred mounted Connecticut soldiers also arrived, they refused to perform any of the duties assigned ordinary soldiers; they saw themselves as "elite" troops.

On July 12, shortly before dawn, a roar of cannon across the harbor announced the arrival of the *Eagle,* Admiral Howe's flagship. It was followed by more than 150 additional vessels carrying redcoats and German soldiers, called Hessians.

Later, a flood tide and a strong wind from the south brought five enemy vessels skimming across the water to the mouth of the Hudson. They included the *Phoenix* with forty guns, the *Rose* with twenty, the schooner *Tryal,* and two tenders.

Drums summoned the Americans to their shore batteries. Few gunners responded. And those who did operate their weapons fired recklessly and harmlessly at the swiftly moving targets.

To the disgust of the commander in chief, hundreds of his soldiers rushed to the shore to gawk at the little fleet. And when the ships went by and continued north, scores followed their progress by running along the riverbank.

For their part, the British let go a few salvos that did no damage but panicked the civilians as cannon balls went rolling and bouncing down the streets.

In General Orders the next day, Washington scolded his men, saying: "Such unsoldierly conduct must grieve every good officer, and give the enemy a mean opinion of the Army, as nothing shows the brave and good soldier more than in case of alarms, coolly and calmly repairing to his post and there waiting orders, whereas a weak curiosity at such a time makes a man look mean and contemptible."

The enemy's quick naval thrust cut a major American communications and supply route. It also demonstrated that the British might now be able to do what Washington dreaded most: push north and forge a linkup with General John "Gentleman Johnny" Burgoyne whenever he chose to march south from Canada.

If that happened, the combined force of the

British would then be strong enough to easily crush the small Northern Army. And that would surely mean the end of America.

One of Washington's many concerns was eased considerably when he learned that Lord Dunmore had left Virginia to join Howe and that, with that danger removed, Martha had left Philadelphia and returned safely to Mount Vernon.

Late in July, he also learned that the Southern Army, in a spectacular and spirited defense, had repulsed General Clinton's attempt to take Charleston with some three thousand men and the support of several ships under Admiral Sir Peter Parker. This welcome news was tempered somewhat at the end of the month when Washington discovered that Clinton and his troops had joined General Howe in New York.

By August 26, 1776, Great Britain had assembled and sent to North America the greatest expeditionary force the world had ever known. And by then, most of it was massed on Long Island only a few miles east of Brooklyn Heights. The objective, Washington predicted, was to destroy the Patriot army with a single stroke and bring an end to America's sudden quest for independence, now but fifty-three days old.

At a hastily called council of war inside the fortifications General Greene had constructed on the Heights, Washington and his officers pieced together the enemy's overall plan:

General Howe's redcoats and Hessians would besiege the Heights, while Admiral Howe's ships would sail into the East River and bombard the Americans from behind. With Washington's army thus engaged, Admiral Howe's ships would also work their way into the East River and bombard American positions in Manhattan.

"They will try to wear us down and expect us to surrender," Washington said grimly as he looked around the conference table. "If we do, the Howes will go up the Hudson to meet Burgoyne."

Yes, the nodding heads indicated, all knew what that meant.

The fortifications atop Brooklyn Heights extended almost two miles in a generally northeast-southwest direction. They consisted of earthworks and crude barricades made of felled trees, rocks, and brush.

The easterly slope, which faced the enemy, was steep, presenting a difficult, but not unsurmountable, obstacle. The wide, level ground below stretched eastward for about a mile, then abruptly rose some fifty feet to a rolling wooded ridge called Guian Heights. Jamaica Road, an uneven slash through dense woods, ran across the crest of the ridge for a distance of about five miles.

Early on the morning of August 27, Washington rode a spirited gray gelding named Tiger to the highest point on Jamaica Road with two aides. When he looked down the far side, he gasped with awe and admiration; for there before him, in a colorful and orderly array, was an army of some 20,000 men, the largest military force he had ever seen!

Hundreds of white tents, arranged in neat rows, added to the spectacle, filling the plain below as far as Washington's eyes could reach. In sharp contrast, too, were the British soldiers in their traditional red uniforms, the German grenadiers in blue, and the jaegers (riflemen) in green, all of whom milled about the tents tending their cook fires and preparing for battle.

At that hour, the greenest third of Washington's total force of 10,000 waited nervously behind the fortifications on Brooklyn Heights. The rest of his puny, unkempt army faced the enemy in positions on high ground among the forested hills farther east; Brigadier General Lord Stirling (also known as William Alexander) was on the right wing near Gowanus Bay with 500 men; General John Sullivan was in the center with 2,200 in three positions. At the extreme left end of Jamaica Road, considered an unlikely area for an attack, Sullivan had stationed a five-man horse patrol.

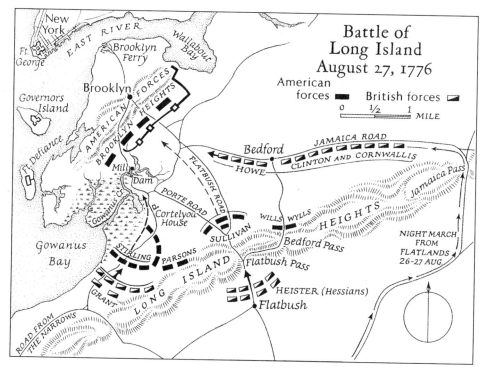

Battle of
Long Island
August 27, 1776

Washington believed that the British would
launch their major attack near Stirling's position
on Gowanus Bay. At daylight it appeared he was
right; British ships opened up on Stirling's troops,
while five thousand redcoats went ashore and
began a steady forward movement.

With Stirling outnumbered ten to one, Washington mounted his horse and rushed all available reinforcements toward his right flank. At about nine
o'clock, however, he heard extremely heavy firing
far off to his left. Washington suddenly realized he
had made a horrible mistake. His army was trapped!

During the night, Generals Cornwallis and Clinton had made an undetected nine-mile march to Jamaica Road with 10,000 men and twenty-eight cannon and captured Sullivan's five-man patrol, silencing a possible alarm.

And while Washington was rushing reinforcements to Stirling on the right, the Hessians bombarded Sullivan's front, but made no attempt to advance.

In the meantime, Cornwallis and Clinton had moved stealthily in behind Sullivan. At nine o'clock, they fired two signal cannon. Now, the Hessians came up the hills and through the woods to attack Sullivan head-on.

Within a few hours an enemy juggernaut was moving on American positions from three different directions.

As Howe's trap closed, hundreds were captured, including Sullivan, Stirling, and several other officers. And while many fought bravely, many more panicked, dropped their guns, and ran for the safety of Brooklyn Heights.

More than 1,400 Americans were killed or wounded, and more than 1,100 captured. The British and Germans, on the other hand, suffered fewer than 400 casualties among a force of 22,000.

In its first stand-up battle, Washington's army had suffered an ignominious defeat.

Strangely, the enemy did not follow up its advantage and storm the fort atop Brooklyn Heights. Instead, with a precision and order that Washington had to admire, the British and Germans moved to positions just out of gunshot range, raised their tents, built cooking fires, and settled down for the night.

Inside the fort was confusion and chaos as the few officers who were left struggled to bury the dead, care for the sick and wounded, and feed the troops. To add to the army's difficulty, scores of farmers and their families, along with their livestock, had rushed into the Heights as soon as the shooting started earlier in the day. They, too, had to be cared for.

Washington spent most of the night moving about the camp trying to make order out of disorder, bolstering defenses, comforting the wounded, and calming the distressed farmers. Shortly before dawn, however, he called his seven remaining senior officers to a council to discuss the army's predicament.

"They're in no hurry," he said. "My guess is that they'll wait until they can get some of their ships behind us before they begin a siege."

At dawn the next day, Washington heard the cry he had long expected: "Sail Ho!"

With telescope in hand, he rushed to a high point on the ramparts. "Look there!" the lookout said, pointing west through the gray morning mist.

Sure enough, six British ships had left their anchorage in Gowanus Bay and were sailing slowly north toward the East River.

Washington now turned his attention to the enemy below. As anticipated, several big guns were being wheeled into position in a long line and tilted up toward the Heights.

A sporadic bombardment began about noon, as though the enemy were testing the range. But just as it did, Washington was again summoned by the lookout.

"They're turning, sir!" the lookout said happily. "The wind's changed to the northeast."

"What a beautiful sight," Washington murmured as the six ships, in perfect formation, turned to port and ran before the wind, their voyage canceled.

On the afternoon of August 29, Washington's Headquarters buzzed with activity as messengers raced to the ferry landing and back.

Soon the troops on Brooklyn Heights heard they were being replaced by fresh units from New York and New Jersey. Officers confirmed the rumors, but warned those who inquired that the exchange had to be made with the utmost quiet and secrecy; or the British might become suspicious and mount an attack that would force a cancellation of the transfer. By late afternoon, the entire force—delighted at the prospect of getting off the Heights and back to the safety of Manhattan—was fully informed.

Throughout the day, Washington's army was divided into units of roughly equal size. At midnight, one by one, each unit marched stealthily to the ferry landing.

On their arrival they found a flotilla of small boats awaiting them. The boats, however, were empty!

"Where are the replacements?" one soldier whispered to his captain.

"What replacements?" the captain asked in mock astonishment.

By 7 A.M. on August 30, thanks to Washington's brilliant lie, his entire army had been moved off Brooklyn Heights and across the East River to Manhattan. The only thing left behind were two heavy cannons mired in mud and several straw dummies perched on the ramparts where Washington's sentries normally stood.

Among those aboard the last flatboat to leave was the commander in chief and his mud-splattered mount, Tiger. As his boat pulled away from the landing, Washington heard shouts from above.

"We've been discovered," he said with a wry smile.

Those around him, and in the heavily loaded

boats nearby, heard the remark, and one soldier cried out, "Oh, ain't that too bad?"

The weary, wet troops roared with laughter. And well they should have, for they now realized that if the enemy had discovered their withdrawal at any time during the night, it would have stormed the Heights. And since the Americans were badly outnumbered, the result of an attack could have been disastrous, especially if hundreds were on the water crossing to New York.

In what was surely one of the greatest deceptions in military history, however, Washington had, in only seven hours, safely removed some 12,000 men from under the very noses of a powerful enemy.

"Burn the town and leave it!" That was General Nathanael Greene's opinion after the army was evacuated from Long Island and, a day later, from Governor's Island.

After a council debate, however, it was decided that New York City would not be set afire and that nine thousand men under General William Heath and all of the army's supplies were to be moved north to Fort Washington on the east bank of the Hudson and to Harlem Heights at the north end of Manhattan Island.

Until this was accomplished, five thousand soldiers would remain in the city under General Israel Putnam, while five brigades were assigned to Greene to repel any attempted British landings along the banks of the East and Hudson rivers.

Washington then quickly shifted Headquarters north to the home of Colonel Roger Morris on Harlem Heights near King's Bridge. It was a timely move; British ships, loaded with troops, were already maneuvering in the waters around Manhattan.

At about 11 A.M. on September 15, the thunder of heavy guns caught Washington's attention. Looking south from Headquarters, he saw a thick column of black smoke float upward midway along the east side of Manhattan at a place called Kip's Bay.

"Those are ship's guns," he said. "It may be a feint, or may be the real thing."

When the bombardment, mounted by the mighty *Phoenix* and five other vessels, continued without letup, Washington was convinced a landing was imminent and rushed to the area.

On reaching Kip's Bay, he came on a scene that filled him with disgust, rage, and shame: Hundreds of panic-stricken Americans were fleeing the enemy without firing a shot!

"Stand! Stand and fight!" he cried repeatedly as he flogged the backs of his troops with the flat of his sword.

Recognizing him, a small group halted and turned toward the enemy, but not for long. When the Hessians bayoneted two of their comrades who had raised their arms in surrender, the Americans turned and ran.

Deserted by their own men, Washington and his aides suddenly found themselves facing an advancing horde of enemy soldiers only a hundred yards away. There was only one thing they could do: Retreat.

As they did so, Washington had to accept a humiliating fact. New York was lost.

F̲our days later, Washington was called from his bed by a member of the Headquarters Guard.

"The town is on fire, sir!" the soldier said.

Washington scrambled into his clothes and rushed outside. Sure enough, far off to the south, he could see a red glow in the sky.

The fire, it was learned later, broke out in a house near the tip of Manhattan Island. A brisk southerly wind had scattered burning shingles among scores of the wooden houses, causing the fire to spread rapidly.

By the time the fire was brought under control, five hundred houses had been destroyed—houses that would have given shelter to redcoats and hundreds of Tories returning to New York now that the city was in the hands of the British.

Although pleased about the fire, Washington was shocked at the report he received the next day from a young artillery captain named Alexander Hamilton.

Hamilton, a sharp-eyed, slender man, said that a British officer had entered his lines under a white flag with a message for the general.

"A message?" Washington asked.

"Yes, sir," Hamilton said. "One of our officers, Nathan Hale, was captured on Long Island, condemned as a spy, and hanged without a trial."

"Damn!" was all a distressed Washington could say as he paced around his office. The twenty-four-year-old Hale had been one of his most promising officers.

When Washington had asked for a captain to volunteer for an intelligence mission within enemy lines on Long Island, Hale was the only man to step forward. Dressed as a school teacher, Hale had left Washington's camp in Harlem Heights on September 12. On his return nine days later, he was captured.

Although Hale was accused of having set the fire that swept through the city, there was no evidence to link him to the conflagration. "Whoever set the fire," Washington said, "has done us a favor by delaying an attack on our lines."

Still, he knew the attack would come.

As Washington predicted, the fire forced a delay in British plans to pursue and destroy his army. The respite gave him time to dash off a series of letters to Congress and to friends and family.

In each, the theme was the same: Unless drastic changes were made in the way the army was supplied and governed, the war could not be won. He pleaded with Congress to increase pay for both privates and officers and to establish a permanent army.

"A good bounty should be immediately offered [to enlistees], aided by the proffer of at least 100, or 150 acres of land and a suit of clothes and a blanket to each non-commissioned officer and soldier."

Current pay for his troops, he said, was "barely sufficient" to keep them in clothes, "much less afford support to their families."

He then underscored the futility of trying to conduct the war with militia from the various colonies. "To place any dependence on militia is, assuredly, resting on a broken staff," he said. "Men just dragged from the tender scenes of domestic life, unaccustomed to the din of arms; totally unacquainted with every kind of military skill, which being a want of confidence in themselves, when opposed to troops regularly trained, disciplined, and appointed, superior in their knowledge and superior in arms, makes them timid and ready to fly from their own shadows."

Washington's "official" letters almost always reflected a passionate concern for his army and "the cause." Some of those to friends and family were equally full of vexation and, often, of anger.

In a letter to his cousin Lund Washington, for example, he said, "In confidence, I tell you that I never was in such an unhappy, divided state since I was born!"

He made one point clear, however: He would not resign.

"If the men stand by me . . . I am resolved not to be forced from this ground while I have life." His resolve was soon sorely tested.

Washington's complaints finally brought a reaction from Congress. Among the positive steps were these:

- Eighty-eight battalions were to be raised by the various states for the duration of the war.
- Each private and noncommissioned officer who enlisted was to receive twenty dollars and one hundred acres of land.
- New articles of war were adopted to improve discipline.
- Officers' pay was increased.
- A full year's supply of clothing and a blanket was to be given to every man.

Washington was stunned to learn, however, that special "commissioners" from each state would have sole authority to choose officers for the new battalions. It may or may not have been obvious to the general, but many members of Congress were fearful that should Washington get too much power he might, when peace was declared, become a dictator.

Washington's concerns were eased by an exchange of prisoners with the British on the basis of ". . . officer for officer of equal rank, soldier for soldier and citizen for citizen. . . ." Among those who happily arrived in camp were Generals John Sullivan and Lord Stirling.

And later, after receiving the thanks of Congress for his efforts in Charleston, a scrawny, unkempt general astride a bony black mare, followed by a pair of scruffy dogs, also rode into Washington's Headquarters—Charles Lee.

On October 12, British transports and warships sailed up the East River and landed a body of troops near what is now The Bronx. Soon afterward other vessels, aided by a favoring tide and wind, whipped up the Hudson past Fort Washington on the east bank and Fort Lee (originally named Independence) on the west, again cutting off communications and supplies.

To avoid entrapment, Washington moved his army quickly and expertly north toward White Plains and left General Greene in command of Fort Washington, which he hoped could be held.

At Chatterton's Hill, just west of White Plains, Washington's men were throwing up earthworks when two columns of the enemy suddenly appeared, set up their artillery, and opened fire.

The second shot hit a militiaman in the thigh and caused him to scream. At that, the entire force turned tail and ran! Chatterton's Hill was lost.

Soon it began to rain heavily. The redcoats promptly took to their tents.

In spite of what this caricature suggests, British expatriate General Charles Lee had more military experience than any other officer in the Patriot Army. Some believed that if he had been born in the Colonies, Congress would have elected him commander in chief instead of Washington. Unfortunately, his ego often got the better of his judgment.

When Howe's troops awoke the next day, the Americans were gone. Washington had moved his entire army and supplies to higher and safer ground at nearby North Castle.

Howe quickly followed, pitching camp only a few miles below the American lines. For five days, as it got colder and colder, the two armies remained motionless but watchful.

At dawn on November 5, a scout galloped his horse up to Washington's tent and called out, "The enemy is leaving!"

Washington promptly called a council of war to discuss strategy. Since the enemy's next move could be to the north, east, or west, Washington, with the concurrence of his officers, decided on a risky maneuver: He divided his army.

Greene would continue to command the garrisons at Forts Lee and Washington. General Lee would remain at North Castle with seven thousand troops. General Heath would be thirty miles upriver in the Hudson Highlands with seven thousand troops, and Washington would cross to New Jersey with at least two thousand men. Washington was confident that troops from any one commander could be quickly moved to support another if needed.

There was, however, a major flaw in this plan.

"Oh, General! Why would you be over-persuaded by men of inferior judgment to your own?" So wrote the outspoken General Lee to his commander.

Washington had, indeed, been persuaded, against

his better judgment, to go along with the decision of a subordinate—a decision that resulted in yet another disaster for the American army. The subordinate was General Greene. The disaster was the loss of Fort Washington.

After three more British ships sailed virtually untouched past the defenses of Fort Lee and Fort Washington, Washington warned Greene that it would be hazardous to leave men and stores at Fort Washington.

Greene replied, "I cannot conceive the garrison to be in any great danger. The men can be brought off at any time."

He was wrong. Overwhelmed by superior numbers and firepower, the American garrison surrendered. And when Fort Washington fell, 2,800 men were taken prisoner and the Patriots lost some of their most valuable cannon and a huge supply of stores. It was, obviously, a staggering defeat.

Typically, General Lee bragged that he "foresaw and predicted everything that happened."

Without letup, the string of defeats pounded through Washington's mind: Long Island, Kip's Bay, Chatterton's Hill, Fort Washington.

In each case, the story was the same: His men refused to fight!

To his brother Jack (John Augustine), he said: "I am wearied almost to death with the retrograde motions of things, and I solemnly protest that twenty-thousand pounds a year would not induce me to undergo what I do. . . ."

A report from the north, however, suddenly boosted his spirits. With a flotilla of small boats hastily built with green timber, Benedict Arnold had fought a critical battle with a squadron of British ships west of Valcour Island on Lake Champlain.

Although he lost the battle, Arnold had blunted an attempt to capture Fort Ticonderoga and forced the enemy into winter quarters. "Do you know what this means?" Washington cried as he broke the news to his staff. "It means that Burgoyne cannot meet Howe until at least next year!" If only, he thought, the army had more officers like Arnold!

Four days later, General Greene sent an urgent message from Fort Lee to Washington's Headquarters east of the Hackensack River: "A farmer just rode in with word that some six thousand of the enemy boarded two hundred boats at Dobbs Ferry and crossed the Hudson early this morning. They are now six miles away and marching toward us at a fast pace."

Thanks to that early warning, Washington was able to help Greene with the hasty evacuation of the fort. He then led a combined force of some 2,500 men toward Newark, New Jersey.

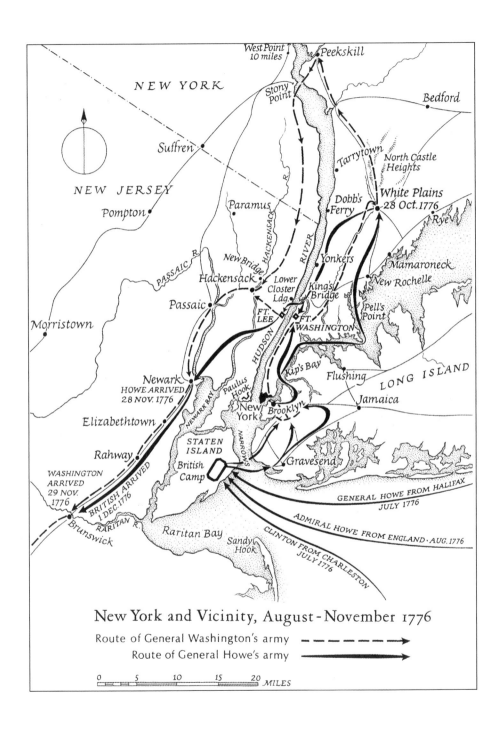

New York and Vicinity, August-November 1776

Route of General Washington's army – – – – ➤
Route of General Howe's army ─────➤

0   5   10   15   20 MILES

Having failed to surprise the Americans, the British camped after following them for only a mile or two.

Once again, Washington had escaped entrapment virtually unscathed. His troops, however, left Fort Lee and his Hackensack camp so hurriedly they had to abandon three hundred tents, their baggage, a thousand barrels of flour, the tools used for digging trenches, and much of their artillery. Only the ammunition was saved.

The war, Washington realized, had arrived in New Jersey. Now, he must unite his army.

Reports from Washington's spies clearly indicated that General Howe planned to march through New Jersey and on to Philadelphia.

This meant a major battle, one the army could not possibly survive without reinforcements. After pulling together all of the troops west of the Hudson, Washington had only 4,400 men; and not all of them were fit for duty. General Lord Cornwallis, on the other hand, already had Washington outnumbered two to one and would soon be picking up reinforcements.

"Keep in mind," General Greene said during a council discussion, "two thousand will be going home in ten days because their enlistments are up.

And in January—if we last that long—hundreds more will leave."

After a somber silence, someone asked, "Is Lee ever going to join us?"

"That's a good question," Washington answered.

Early in November, when Washington divided his army into four parts, he sent the following note to General Lee at White Plains: "If the enemy should remove the whole, or the greatest part of their force, to the west side of the Hudson River, I have no doubt of your following with all possible dispatch. . . ." Despite the polite language, that was an order.

But even though Lee knew about the capture of Fort Lee and the buildup of British forces, he remained where he was with seven thousand of the best and most experienced men; an army larger than the one now under Washington's direct command.

Toward the end of November, Washington again ordered Lee to join him. When Lee failed to respond, a third order followed.

Finally, Lee agreed to "endeavor" to put Washington's orders "in execution," but he questioned "whether I shall be able to carry with me any considerable number of men, not so much from a want of zeal in the men as from their wretched condition with respect to shoes, stockings, etc . . ."

Luckily, bad weather held up a British advance. When it cleared on November 28, Cornwallis began to press forward, forcing Washington south to Brunswick.

On December 1, Cornwallis was only ten miles behind Washington's fleeing troops. Unconcerned, hundreds of Flying Camp militiamen (soldiers and horsemen who could move fast to where they might be needed) left for home.

When the militiamen departed, Washington's orders were crisp and clear: "We will continue our retreat across the Raritan River and go on to Princeton where, it is hoped, we will be joined by General Lee and his troops."

After marching across a bridge that spanned the Raritan, the Americans burned it, bringing an abrupt but temporary halt to the British advance.

On December 3, what was left of Washington's little army arrived in Trenton, boarded a flotilla of boats of every size and description and crossed the Delaware River to Pennsylvania.

There was still no sign of Lee, nor any word from him. The situation for the Americans was now becoming desperate for several reasons. An attempt to coax more recruits out of the governor of New Jersey had failed, and a similar effort in Philadelphia had been only partly successful.

Convinced that the British were about to win the war, thousands in New Jersey quickly responded to an offer by General Howe of "Royal Forgiveness," swore allegiance to the King, and pocketed Royal pardons.

Suppliers of flour and other goods for Washing-

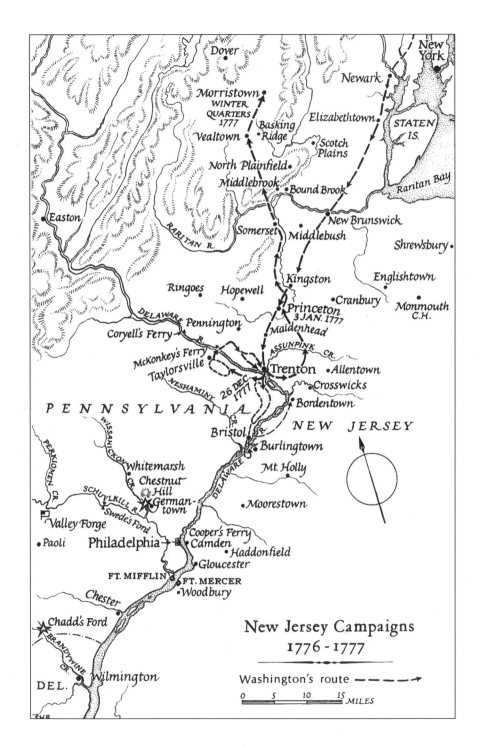

New Jersey Campaigns
1776-1777

Washington's route ------>

0   5   10   15 MILES

ton's army refused to fill orders because they feared that colonial paper money was worthless.

And on January 1—just three weeks away—Washington would need a new army, just as he had in Boston at the end of 1775.

At a tense council during the first week of December, Washington focused on the principal problem. "I am still convinced they mean to take Philadelphia," he said soberly.

All agreed. And all knew that if Howe beat them and Philadelphia fell, the war was lost.

On December 8, Lee sent Washington two letters. In both, he tried to persuade Washington that he would be more useful attacking the British rear.

Washington had had enough. He sent Colonel Stephen Moylan to Morristown to deliver the following message to General Lee: "All the general officers with me agree that you should join me with your whole force with all possible speed. . . . If you arrive without delay we may be able to preserve Philadelphia, whose loss would be fatal to the cause of America."

After delivering that order, Moylan was to hurry on to the Northern Army and order General Gates to also join Washington with reinforcements as soon as possible. To many, the army now bogged down in Pennsylvania seemed about to collapse, taking with it all hope that the United States, now only eighteen months old, would survive.

Underscoring a growing public despondency that came close to panic were these developments:

- Hundreds of civilians continued to declare their allegiance to the Crown.
- The New Jersey legislature disbanded, its members going into hiding.
- On December 13, Congress fled to Baltimore.

Until ordered otherwise, Congress said Washington "should be possessed of full power to order and direct all things relative to the department, and to the operations of the war." The committee relaying this order to Washington added: "Happy it is for this country that the General of their forces can safely be entrusted with the most unlimited power, and neither personal security, liberty, or property be in the least degree endangered thereby."

While all this was encouraging, Washington still believed he needed General Lee at his side to stave off an attack on Philadelphia. But where was Lee?

On December 12, Lee rode out of his camp near Basking Ridge, New Jersey, to visit one of several women at White's Tavern, which was five miles away, and spent the night. He was unable or unwilling to come down from the bedroom to the floor below until late the next morning. When he did, he wore only his pants, a dirty undershirt, and a pair of slippers.

"General," a nervous aide said, "hadn't we best get back to camp?"

"I'll go when I'm damned good and ready," was Lee's surly reply. "Right now, I'm going to have breakfast. Then I've got to write a letter to Gates."

At about ten o'clock, Lee wolfed down the breakfast prepared by the widow who owned the tavern and began to write his letter. Just as he signed it, his aide rushed in and said, "We've been surrounded by British cavalry!"

"Where's the guard?" Lee shouted. "Damned guard, why don't they shoot?"

"They've been captured," was the reply.

"Cowards!" Lee roared.

The widow took Lee by the arm. "Come, you'd better hide," she said.

"Where?"

"Upstairs under the bed!"

"Nonsense!" Lee said.

"In the closet then!"

Lee rushed up the stairs behind the widow. She pushed him into a closetlike space above the fireplace but, small as he was, he wouldn't fit.

It didn't matter. They both heard the order: "If the general does not surrender in five minutes, I'll burn the house!"

The general surrendered.

When last seen that day, the man who hoped to replace Washington was flying toward the enemy lines aboard his aide's horse in the company of five dragoons. According to the aide, he was bareheaded and still in slippers and trousers. A "blanket coat," however, was thrown over his shirt, "very much soiled from several days use."

The aide managed to send Lee's letter to Gates. In it Lee again complained about the loss of Fort Washington. "There never was so damned a stroke," he said, adding, ". . . a certain great man is damnably deficient."

Two days later, when his troops joined Washington across the Delaware, Lee was in captivity in Brunswick.

The "damnably deficient great man," however, would hear from him again.

Toward the end of the year, Washington decided he must stop running and go on the offensive. His rationale was sound: When enlistments expired on January 1, 1777, the army would be in its weakest state, a condition that would surely invite the enemy to again come after him. The plan developed in council seemed simple enough: The army would attack the British outposts on the New Jersey side of the Delaware River on December 25,

Christmas Day. The day was deliberately selected because it was well known that the Hessians traditionally celebrated the occasion with feasting and heavy drinking.

Washington, Greene, and Sullivan would cross the Delaware River at McKonkey's Ferry (now Washington's Crossing), nine miles above Trenton, a village of some one hundred houses. With them would be 2,400 troops and 18 cannon. At an agreed-to time, this force would approach Trenton from the north. John Glover's Marblehead Regiment would run the boats for the crossing. Double-ended Durham boats, sixty feet long and eight feet wide, would carry most of the men and artillery. Shaped somewhat like canoes, these boats drew little water and could carry up to fifteen tons of cargo. To propel them, seamen jabbed and pushed long poles into the river bottom from narrow decks that ran the length of the boats on either side. The crossing was to start at dark and be completed by midnight. After a rest, Washington's troops would march in a southwesterly direction to Trenton, arriving there at dawn.

General James Ewing, with 1,000 militia, would cross at Trenton Ferry and take a position south of the town on the banks of Assunpink Creek, while General John Cadwalader and another 1,800 militia would cross the Delaware farther south and attack the enemy garrisons at Burlington and Bordentown. To maintain the element of surprise, every effort would be made to silence sentries before an alarm could be given, or a shot fired.

Just as Washington was about to lead his men out of the Pennsylvania camp at two o'clock on Christmas Day, he discovered that General Gates, who had only recently arrived in camp with a large body of troops, was not available.

"Where is he?" Washington asked.

"In Philadelphia," one of Gates's aides responded, "discussing matters concerning the Northern Command." Washington was now about to go into battle without the services of the army's two most experienced generals, Lee and Gates. As usual, he buried his personal feelings and clamped his mind on the task at hand. But, almost from the beginning, things began to go wrong.

One by one, in freezing weather, the boats and barges were loaded at McConkey's Ferry with men, horses, and artillery.

And one by one, Glover's men poled their heavy cargoes across the shallow, icy river as those aboard, with sticks and gun butts, did their best to ward off the hundreds of swiftly moving ice floes that threatened their safety.

Washington was among the very first to reach the Jersey shore. Within the hour, however, weather conditions deteriorated rapidly. The temperature plunged, and it began to snow. Worse yet, the wind grew to gale force, punctuated by fierce gusts.

Shielding his face from the blizzard as he peered anxiously into the darkness, Washington told an aide, "If everyone doesn't get across, we'll have to go back as soon as the storm blows out."

The operation had become extremely dangerous. Several times, wind gusts tilted the barges enough to cause the horses aboard to lose their footing and the heavy guns to shift so violently that only the most strenuous efforts of the soldiers kept them from going overboard.

The vicious wind also pelted the boats and men with river water that was now beginning to freeze. This made slippery footing for those poling the boats and caused the clothes of all aboard to stiffen and become as inflexible as boards.

As originally calculated, the crossing was to be completed by midnight. But the last boat didn't reach the Jersey shore until 3 A.M.

When it did, a downhearted Washington remarked, as though talking to himself, "It will be impossible to reach Trenton before daybreak."

He said no more, but his officers knew what he was thinking: They might not catch the enemy by surprise, after all. And an attempt to attack such a strong post in broad daylight could end in disaster, especially with a force that had never shown much of an inclination to fight.

But there was no turning back.

The troops went quietly along a road that followed the river until it forked at a place called Birmingham. There, at daybreak, the order to halt was passed back to the long, cold, and weary column.

Calling his officers together, Washington said in a low voice, "According to our intelligence we are now about five miles from the town."

Then, pointing to a snow-covered depression to his left, he added, "That should be Pennington Road. General Greene, you and I will take it so we can approach the town from the north. General Sullivan, you will continue on River Road. This will bring you into the town from the west. We should attack together, starting at approximately eight o'clock. If you encounter the enemy before then, don't wait. Enter the town as quickly as possible. Agreed?"

After a nodding of heads, the officers synchronized their timepieces. When all were ready, Washington said, "Let's move on, gentlemen. And good luck!"

Whispered orders were quickly passed to the troops: "March! No talking! No lights."

Followed by three infantry regiments, a small troop of Philadelphia Light Horse, and nine pieces of artillery, Washington and Greene led the way along Pennington Road. Sullivan, with three regiments and nine guns, continued down River Road.

At eight o'clock, Washington's men came on a Hessian outpost at the northern end of the village.

As they moved forward they heard a shout. They were spotted!

Twenty enemy soldiers burst out of a small building and began firing and falling back toward the center of Trenton.

Slipping and sliding on the ice and snow, the Americans quickly followed. With extraordinary effort in the freezing weather, the gunners placed their heavy, cumbersome cannon wheel-to-wheel at the heads of two straight, parallel streets (King and Queen Streets) that ran south through the center of the town for a distance of about a half mile.

Boom! Boom! Boom! Boom!

The roar of the cannon immediately lifted the spirits of the Americans. "Beautiful music, ain't it?" one snow-covered soldier called out to another.

Sullivan's troops, meanwhile, routed fifty Hessians from an outpost at the western edge of Trenton. This group also opened fire and fell back before the advancing Americans.

While pressing on from the west, Sullivan sent a large body of troops to the southern edge of Trenton to block the foot of Queen Street where it led to a bridge over Assunpink Creek, shutting off an escape route for the Hessians.

Soon, the entire enemy force of some 1,200 men were in the streets trying to fight off the attackers. Four cannon were wheeled into place on King and Queen Streets, aimed into the teeth of the howling wind and snow, and fired, but to no effect. Before the guns could be loaded a second time, artillery under the command of Captain Alexander Hamilton boomed out and silenced the Hessian pieces.

The Americans charged into the town from every direction, forcing the Hessians into an open area to the east where they tried to form a battle line. Although he had positioned himself on high ground, Washington could see little through the wind-whipped snow.

Suddenly, a young mounted American officer galloped to his side and yelled, "Sir, they struck their colors!"

The enemy had surrendered.

For various reasons related to the storm, Generals Ewing and Cadwalader were unable to make a successful crossing of the Delaware and attack their assigned targets. Still, in less than two hours, Washington had won his first and most important victory. His reports from commanders showed that not a single American had lost his life in the engagement at Trenton. Four were wounded, however, including an eighteen-year-old lieutenant named James Monroe (who would become America's fifth president). And during the rest after the crossing, two men had fallen asleep and were frozen to death.

By contrast, 25 or 30 Hessians were killed, many more were wounded, and 918 were taken prisoner. Also captured were a thousand stand of arms, several cannon, wagons, horses, powder and shot, and other supplies.

Because the enemy forces at Princeton, Burlington, and Bordentown were well rested and Washington's troops were tired after their all-night march and the strain of battle, the decision was made that the army would recross the Delaware with the prisoners and the spoils.

Starting about noon, Washington and his men returned to McConkey's Ferry, this time covering the nine miles with the wild northwest wind driving snow and sleet into their bent heads and faces with stinging force.

And when they clambered stiffly into the boats, they found the river more hazardous than it had been the night before—higher, faster, and filled with more of the dangerous ice floes. Still, the army, without sleep or rest for a day and two nights, arrived back at their camp at noon the following day in high spirits.

While his men slept, Washington doggedly stayed awake long enough to send a report to Congress: "I have the pleasure of congratulating you upon the success of an enterprise which I had formed against a detachment of the enemy lying in Trenton, and which was executed yesterday morning." After describing what happened, he said that if Ewing and Cadwalader had been able to join him, he would have driven the enemy out of all their posts east and south of Trenton.

He also praised his troops, saying: "In justice to the officers and men, I must add that their behavior upon this occasion reflects the highest honor upon them. The difficulty of passing the river in a very severe night, and their march through a violent storm of snow and hail did not in the least abate their ardor. But when it came to the charge, each seemed to vie with the other in pressing forward. . . ."

To the men themselves, his "victory message" was even more laudatory. He followed it up by ordering a round of rum for his troops along with the news that the booty would be evaluated and shared among those "who crossed the river." Unfortunately, rum, praise, and a division of captured supplies did not fill the army's greatest need: food. The commissary was so low on food that the troops were immediately put on short rations.

Then came two pieces of exciting and unexpected news. Encouraged by the victory at Trenton, militiamen from Pennsylvania, New England, and Virginia were on the way. And Cadwalader had crossed the Delaware with 1,500 men. He suggested that Washington bring his troops over and, together, they could "beat up" the British posts and "keep up the panic" created by the victory at Trenton. Yes! Washington thought. What a marvelous opportunity!

But disturbing questions arose in council. Suppose the river froze but would not be solid enough to bear the weight of the men and artillery? What then? Could the men be expected to go through another crossing without food in their bellies? What could be done about the men whose enlistments were up on the first of January? There were no immediate answers.

The army rose from its bed on December 29 and began a slow, winding move toward the Delaware—a march through six to eight inches of snow in extreme cold.

Because ice extended into the river from each shore, the crossing took longer and was more difficult than it had been on Christmas night. By the morning of December 30, however, some five thousand Americans were camped on high ground south of Trenton, just beyond the bridge that crossed Assunpink Creek.

Shivering in the cold the next day, the ragged, bearded, unkempt regiments scheduled to leave the army formed several lines shoulder-to-shoulder to hear Washington's last words.

Astride Snowman, a magnificent white charger that stood more than seventeen hands high, the general rode slowly along the front line to the center, then turned his mount so both faced the troops. Relaxed and smiling, the soldiers stared boldly at the general. Soon they would be free of the suffering and hunger; free to return to the warmth of their homes and families.

Washington began to speak in a voice that carried easily to every ear. "Gentlemen," he said, "you have served your country well these past few days. You deserve every honor, every accolade a grateful public can bestow upon you. Now, your time is up. Of that, there is no question.

"But the great victory you won—there, just beyond the bridge behind you—does not mean the end of the war."

Then, in a louder, stronger tone, he said, "Within a few days, thousands of militiamen will be joining us. Raw recruits! Men of tender years who have never faced an enemy with a gun or bayonet. These new men will not stay with us if you, combat veterans of the Continental Army, are not at their side. And so, I ask you, in the name of the United States, in the name of your country and all you treasure, re-enlist. Re-enlist now! Today!"

The men shifted uneasily, their eyes no longer on Washington's face, but off to the left, the right, toward the clouds, or directed at the ground.

"Six weeks," Washington called out in a voice tinged with emotion. "If you are willing to stay six weeks, I am prepared to pay a bounty of ten dollars. Ten dollars for service in the cause of liberty and justice!"

The men were unimpressed. Washington's tone changed. "Can it be that you are not aware of all that is happening to that part of your country in the hands of the enemy? Can it be that you have not heard of the pillaging of farms, homes and places of business? Even the property of the feck-less who have turned their backs on us and sworn allegiance to the king? And what of the atrocities? The brutal rapes of innocent women; females as young as seven, as old as seventy?

"Do not delude yourself. Your property and your wife, sister, and mother are not safe if we are conquered. Is it not worth ten dollars to give up the chimney corner for six more weeks? Or until we build an army strong enough to drive the enemy from our shores?" After another pause, he said, "Gentlemen, I beseech you, consider your answer carefully."

Washington now rode to the side of the line and ordered the drums to beat for volunteers. The men, however, seemed frozen in place.

Washington rode Snowman forward and again faced his men. "Shall it be slavery or liberty?" he shouted. At his signal, the drums rolled noisily a second time.

Suddenly, a bearded soldier in a floppy black hat stepped forward. Jabbing the muzzle of his musket skyward, he yelled, "I say Liberty!"

Like an ocean wave, the lines surged ahead as the soldiers raised their weapons and cried repeat-edly, "Liberty! Liberty!"

At dawn on January 2, Washington received a message from one of his Patriot spies: "Cornwallis left Princeton early this morning with a large body of troops and headed down Post Road for Trenton. Moving fast."

Washington's position was both strong and weak. Strong because Assunpink Creek was in front of him on low ground. Weak because the Delaware was at his back and his boats were far upriver.

On receiving the message, Washington rushed several units out along the Princeton–Trenton road toward the oncoming redcoats with this order: "Delay the enemy's approach to the bridge until dark."

The delaying action was remarkably successful; the British were unable to reach the bridge until dusk. And when an attempt was made to storm it, Washington's artillery easily broke the charge.

Cornwallis, confident of victory the next day, pitched camp for the night. Washington seemed to do the same. All along the creek across from the enemy's lines, his campfires burned brightly.

At daylight, however, the British discovered "the fox," as Washington had become known to enemy commanders, had slipped away again.

Using a map of the Princeton area that Cadwalader had received from a Patriot spy, Washington had moved his troops well to the east before crossing Assunpink Creek.

At daylight, he led his troops toward Princeton along a little-used back road that ran parallel to Post Road, the main road out of Princeton.

At eight o'clock, Washington sent General Hugh Mercer, one of his best officers, to the left with 350 men to destroy a bridge on Post Road.

The objective was to hamper Cornwallis when he tried to come after the Americans. Destruction of the bridge would also close an escape route from Princeton.

At about 8:30, Washington heard a fusillade of shots to his left. Alarmed, he rushed a regiment of Cadwalader's militiamen toward the sound of battle.

"Faster!" he shouted at the running men. In the distance, he saw Mercer and his troops retreating through an orchard, pursued by a large body of redcoats.

Sending for reinforcements, Washington continued toward the fray, arriving just as Mercer fell from his horse, mortally wounded.

With their leader down, most of Mercer's men began to flee. Just then, however, two cannons under command of Captain Joseph Moulder halted the enemy in their tracks.

By now, Cadwalader, Greene, and Colonel Daniel Hitchcock had arrived and rallied the Americans. With Washington alone in front of a long battle line, the Americans began a steady advance toward the unflinching British.

"Don't fire until you hear my command!"

Washington shouted, drawing his sword and raising it above his head.

When the lines were but thirty yards apart, Washington, with bullets whining and whistling around him, swept his blade downward and cried, "Fire!"

Suddenly, the British line broke and scattered. A jubilant Washington, his sword raised, galloped after the fleeing redcoats and disappeared.

Following the battle, Washington's officers and troops were busy rounding up prisoners, the wounded, the dead, and the artillery pieces the British had left behind when someone exclaimed in alarm, "Where is His Excellency?"

No one knew.

"My God! He's been killed!" an officer cried.

But, no. There, cantering across a wide field toward them came Washington, a bright smile on his face. "It was a fine fox chase, my boys!" he called out, sparking laughter and cheers.

The army continued its march into Princeton where it found a small enemy force holed up in Nassau Hall, a fifty-two room college building situated in the center of the town. A blast from one of Captain Alexander Hamilton's guns flushed them out. Collecting more prisoners and stores, Washington left Princeton's northern border just as Cornwallis entered the town from the south.

Two days later, Washington's weary, ill-fed, and ill-clad army was spread out over the hills of Morristown. The British, meanwhile, had withdrawn to the north, content to wait until spring for another campaign which might—or might not—be launched against Philadelphia. The only posts left in South Jersey were at Brunswick and Amboy, both of which were soon withdrawn.

For Washington, the winter campaign of 1776–1777 had ended with an incredible reversal. Still, the battle for America's independence had not yet been won.

Washington had never been to Morristown, New Jersey, a village of about fifty houses, a tavern, and two churches. When he arrived there after the Battle of Princeton, however, he quickly became convinced that this was an ideal location for his winter quarters.

Morristown was some thirty miles from New York and about the same distance from British posts at Brunswick, Newark, and Amboy. The hills in and around the town, he decided, would give his troops valuable protection should the British come after him with a superior force. The farms in the area also gave him an abundant supply of food for both men and horses.

Headquarters was in the center of the village in Freeman's Tavern, a small building that was a popular meeting place for Patriots and members of the Masonic Lodge. Two rooms over the bar served as Washington's office and bedroom.

While his "family" of officers were lodged in some of the other buildings in the town, the troops were mostly in log huts deliberately spread over a large area to confuse British spies by creating the impression that the army might be twice its actual size.

The only action in the field during these quiet early months of 1777 were skirmishes with British foraging parties. And while it was comforting to have Martha join him again when the roads became passable, Washington had to contend with a serious administrative headache: Congress had promoted five officers over the head of Benedict Arnold, his favorite fighter.

Arnold, who had been sent to Providence, Rhode Island, to plan a campaign against the enemy in Newport, said in an angry note to Washington that the action by Congress "must be a civil way of asking for my resignation."

Washington responded that he was unaware of the promotions and had not approved them. He asked Arnold not to resign, promising he would do his best "to have this injustice corrected."

In late April 1777, before Washington could act on Arnold's behalf, General Howe sent two thousand men under Governor William Tryon of New York to Danbury, Connecticut, to destroy an important depot of Patriot stores. Arnold was rushed to the scene to lead the local militia against the enemy. But by the time he arrived, the British had burned the town.

As the British troops began to return to their ships, a small force under Arnold and Generals Gold Silliman and David Wooster and Colonel John Lamb gallantly tried to block them at Ridgefield. During the course of the battle, Wooster was killed, while Arnold barely escaped with his life.

This display of bravery and leadership prompted Congress to promote Arnold to major general. While he now had equal rank with the five officers promoted earlier, Congress did not grant him seniority.

In May, Congress also passed this resolution: ". . . that [Arnold] shall have a horse properly caparisoned as a token of their approbation of his gallant conduct in which General Arnold had one horse killed under him and another wounded."

But Arnold was not satisfied.

Twenty years earlier, France had been Washington's enemy in the French and Indian War. Now, because of its continued rivalry with Britain for world dominance, France was a friend.

To Washington's delight, France delivered 6,800 stands of small arms to his army early in 1777. Later, the brig *Sally* arrived in Delaware with 6,000 muskets and 1,500 firelocks, while the French ship *Mercury* landed in Portsmouth, New Hampshire, with 1,200 firelocks, 1,000 barrels of powder, 48 bales of woolens, and several cannon.

But France sent something else that caused a mind-boggling problem: boatloads of military officers. Some of those who strutted into Washington's office in glittering beribboned uniforms, demanding a high-ranking command, were obviously phony. Some were legitimate. And since he didn't speak French, Washington could never be sure of others.

Among those whom Washington welcomed were three expert engineers under command of Colonel Louis le Beque Duportail and Colonel Thomas Conway, an Irishman serving in the French army. Conway was the only foreign officer who could speak English. Congress made Conway a brigadier, a move that Washington would later regret.

Late in the spring of 1777, Howe tried to lure Washington into battle on the plains of New Jersey. When he failed, he abandoned the state. Washington now reasoned that Howe would soon do one of three things: (1) launch an attack against Peekskill to gain control of the Hudson Highlands; (2) wait for General Burgoyne to start his campaign against Ticonderoga, then sail up the Hudson to meet him; or (3) board his ships and head for Philadelphia.

On July 10, Washington received this dispatch from General Schuyler: "Ticonderoga evacuated. Most of garrison captured."

Early the next day—July 11—Congress received Benedict Arnold's resignation from military service. Later the same day, when word spread that Ticonderoga had fallen, Arnold rushed back to Independence Hall and asked that his resignation request be suspended.

When Congress agreed, Arnold set out to join Schuyler. At virtually the same time, General Gates's New England friends in Congress began a campaign to give Gates command of the Northern Army. After two weeks of maneuvering, they succeeded.

Washington, meanwhile, became convinced that Howe would soon try to form a juncture with General Burgoyne. He started his army toward New York in the vicinity of West Point.

On one of Washington's busiest days, however, Alexander Hamilton brought a dirty, bearded man dressed in ragged civilian clothes to Washington's office. "He's a deserter from an enemy brigade stationed in New York harbor," Hamilton said with a knowing look.

"Why did you desert?" Washington asked.

"Cause we was treated like dogs," the ragged man replied angrily. "All day they put us to work in the holds of the ships. It was hotter'n hell and wot we got to eat wasn't fit fer pigs!"

"What kind of work were you doing aboard the ships?"

"Knockin' together walk-in stalls for horses."

Horses? Howe's ships being fitted for horses? "Take care of this man and call a council," Washington barked at Hamilton.

Washington knew, of course, that for an extensive land operation, a large number of horses were needed for officers, and to pull supply wagons and artillery. Scores of horses aboard ship could mean only one thing: Philadelphia, not the upper Hudson, where relatively few horses were necessary, was Howe's objective!

Breaking off the march to West Point, Washington reversed course and led his leg-weary and still poorly clad troops another 150 miles southward.

On July 30, John Hancock wrote the commander that 228 British ships had appeared off the mouth of Delaware Bay.

By the time Washington received this message, he had reached Chester, Pennsylvania, only a few miles from Philadelphia. On the morning of his arrival he also received this word from a boat captain in Delaware Bay: "A large ship which we took to be the *Admiral* fired a gun and immediately the whole Fleet backed and stood off to the eastward. By four o'clock P.M. they were out of sight. . . ."

Thoroughly confused, Washington decided to stay close to Philadelphia and rest his weary men until Howe's next move.

On August 1, yet another foreign officer, commissioned by Congress, arrived at Headquarters and was introduced by Hamilton as, "Marie Joseph Paul Yves Roch Gilbert du Motier, Marquis de Lafayette."

Washington looked the nineteen-year-old Lafayette over carefully as his visitor bowed stiffly and with a shy but warm smile, extended a soft, white hand.

What Washington saw was a nervous young man, slight of build with a narrow face, bright hazel eyes, a rather deep cleft in his chin and a blondish, receding hairline.

Hamilton, who spoke French fluently, explained that Lafayette had joined the French army when he was thirteen and rose to the rank of captain. At sixteen, he married a member of one of the most powerful families in France, a family well-connected to the King's Court.

"He wants to serve as a volunteer at his own expense," Hamilton added.

"Now, Captain, I hope you realize that your appointment is honorary," Washington said during the interview.

"But, *oui*! Yes! *Oui*!" Lafayette beamed after Hamilton translated.

The young nobleman explained through Hamilton that he wanted Washington to know that he had joined his command "to learn."

Washington took an instant liking to Lafayette and promptly announced he would become one of his aides. (Congress had commissioned Lafayette as a major general without command.)

A few days later, the British fleet was sighted off the entrance to Chesapeake Bay. A major test

Courageous and skillful in battle, the Marquis de Lafayette, the youngest of Washington's aides, was like a son to the general.

for the American army—and young Lafayette—would soon be at hand.

On August 25, a hot, muggy day, Howe began to land his troops six miles below Head of Elk (now Elkton, Maryland). His brother, Admiral Richard Howe, it turned out, had balked at sailing his ships up the Delaware to Philadelphia because the shoreline and small islands in the river bristled with fortifications. Tory spies had also told him that underwater obstructions had been placed in the narrower passages, obstructions that could easily hole a ship. As a result, the Howes were now some forty miles south of Philadelphia.

For five days, the British and Hessians concentrated on replenishing their food supplies and rounding up horses and livestock. Scores of large foraging parties scoured the countryside, taking everything and anything of value that they could find.

On September 2, some 12,500 enemy troops began to move northward toward the Brandywine River. And there, blocking the enemy's line of march to Philadelphia, Washington's army lay in waiting.

Washington positioned the main body of his troops about fifteen miles from Philadelphia to the east of the Brandywine River at a place

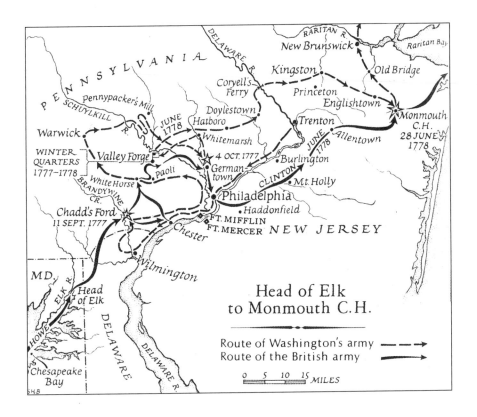

Head of Elk
to Monmouth C.H.

Route of Washington's army ‒ ‒ ‒ →
Route of the British army ━━━→

0   5   10   15   MILES

called Chad's Ford (now Chadd's Ford). This was only a few miles from Kennett Square, where the enemy camped on the night of September 10.

As he looked at a crude map, he could see that there were several places where troops could easily cross the river, which ran in a northwest-southeast direction. Several miles upstream, the small East Branch of the river joined the much larger West Branch at what was called The Forks.

At dawn on September 11, a heavy fog shrouded the area. By eight o'clock, however, a hot sun had burned it off. Washington now heard firing from beyond the west bank of the river.

Soon, he saw his infantry retreating toward him in good order. After his men crossed to the east bank, the enemy brought up several pieces of artillery and opened fire. Henry Knox's guns boomed in response.

By eleven o'clock, Washington was convinced that General Howe was engaging his center only to give him time to turn the American right flank.

Two reports confirmed this belief. One was from Colonel Moses Hazen, who was stationed two and a half miles distant on Washington's right, and the other from Lieutenant Colonel James Ross, who patrolled Valley Road, beyond Hazen.

"If the enemy is above the Forks, Howe has left half his army in front of us," Washington told his staff. After a brief discussion, he reached a decision.

"Gentlemen," he said, "prepare to cross the river and attack."

Just as his men were about to move across Chad's Ford, he received an alarming note from General Sullivan, who was stationed with his troops on the right: ". . . Some of the Militia who came in this morning from . . . the Forks of the Brandywine heard nothing of the Enemy above the Forks. . . . Colonel Hazen's information must be wrong."

If Hazen's information was wrong, Howe's main army was still in front of him, and he could be sending his troops into a trap!

"Hold the men!" he cried to his officers as he galloped a black mare along the riverbank.

Ross and Hazen were correct. Those who had informed Sullivan were wrong.

To extricate the army from the trap now closing on it, Washington rushed Sullivan, Major General Adam Stephen, and Lord Stirling to meet British Generals Cornwallis and Howe on the right at Birmingham Meeting House. He and General Greene, along with Generals William Maxwell and Anthony Wayne remained at Chad's Ford to keep the British in check on the west bank of the Brandywine.

But sitting idle at Headquarters while a battle raged on his right and to the rear became too much for Washington. He ordered Greene to the right to help Sullivan, left Brigadier Benjamin Lincoln to guard Chad's Ford, and, with Lafayette and other aides, galloped toward the sound of gunfire.

Washington arrived at the American front just as the line began to crumble. He and Lafayette rode among the retreating men, trying to rally them.

Bullets were pouring into the American position as the British pressed forward. Washington heard a cry of pain from Lafayette. Seeing blood spurt from the Frenchman's left leg, Washington called to a surgeon, "Take care of this man immediately!"

Fatigue from a seventeen-hour march slowed the British advance. It came to a halt as darkness fell. In the meantime, however, the British charged across Chad's Ford, forcing the troops under Wayne and Maxwell to retreat.

When the attack ended, Washington sent word to all of his officers to take the road to Chester. Arriving there at midnight, he fell into bed. Exhausted, he had an aide write a report to John Hancock, which he approved and signed. "Sir: I am sorry to inform you, that in this day's engagement, we have been obliged to leave the enemy masters of the field.

"Unfortunately the intelligence received of the enemy's advancing up the Brandywine, and crossing at a ford about six miles above us, was uncertain and contradictory, notwithstanding all my pains to get the best. . . ."

He concluded by saying: "Notwithstanding the misfortune of the Army I am happy to find the troops in good spirits; and I hope another time we shall compensate for the losses now sustained."

During the next two days the army covered another twenty-one miles in heavy rain to Redding Furnace, where it was resupplied with ammunition. Washington then led the troops to Yellow Springs (now Chester Springs), then on to the Schuylkill River.

Just before he crossed from the west to the east bank of the Schuylkill, however, Washington called General Wayne to where he sat his horse, a big buckskin aptly named Buck.

"I'm told you lived near here as a boy, is that correct?"

"Yes, sir," Wayne replied.

"Then you know the area well?"

"I do," came the reply.

Washington thought for a moment, then said, "The British are still on the road to Philadelphia. Do you think it is possible to seclude yourself someplace and fall on their rear and perhaps destroy their baggage?"

"Yes, sir, I do," the fiery Wayne responded. "If they continue on the road, they will pass Warren Tavern at the foot of a range of hills. That would be an ideal place to have a go at them."

"Good," Washington said. "And good luck."

Wayne promptly detached his division of 1,500 and four field pieces from the main army. After dark, he moved them to a wooded area about a mile north of Warren Tavern (now Malvern) and two miles southwest of Paoli Tavern. Unfortunately, however, local Tories had spotted Wayne's men and hurried to inform the oncoming British army.

At ten o'clock on the night of September 20, British Major General Charles Grey led three regiments toward Wayne's campsite.

Four sentries posted near Warren Tavern fired

at the rapidly approaching British and ran. The shots aroused Wayne's men, and they formed for battle as quickly as they could.

The light from the campfires behind many of the Americans, however, gave the enemy excellent targets and several were shot down immediately. Others were killed in a bayonet charge.

Satisfied with the results of the attack, Grey called off his men and returned to Howe's army. Wayne somehow escaped with several hundred of his soldiers and his artillery.

Left behind were about 150 Americans killed, captured, or wounded. Forty of the most severely wounded were left in houses along the British line of march. On the field, however, were fifty-three "mangled dead," victims of the cruel bayonets.

When word of the British surprise attack spread, propagandists immediately dubbed it the Paoli Massacre!

Anticipating the loss of Philadelphia, Congress had the foresight to move magazines and all of the army's important stores far to the west and north.

Having crossed to the east bank of the Schuylkill in an attempt to keep his army between the enemy and the city, Washington was startled by a report received on September 21: The British were on the march—away from Philadelphia!

"He's going after our supplies at Redding Furnace," General Greene said. Washington agreed. Within hours, the army was on the march along the east side of the Schuylkill, trying to catch up to Howe on the opposite bank.

Overnight, unknown to the Americans, the British reversed course, crossed the river behind Washington and later marched into the outskirts of Philadelphia without a shot being fired.

Washington had been neatly outmaneuvered.

The capture of Philadelphia, however, was not doomsday, as many—including Washington—had predicted. The main army, although it had dwindled to eight thousand, was still intact. And Congress, after one day in Lancaster, was established in York.

Then came an electrifying report from the Northern Army: Gates (with considerable help from Arnold, who was badly wounded) had won a major battle against Burgoyne's army at Freeman's Farm near Saratoga.

The defeat brought an end to the British goal of establishing a linkup between Howe and Burgoyne which, if accomplished, would have knocked New England out of the war.

In celebration of the "victory," Washington ordered all troops to be paraded and a gill of rum to be given each man. He also inaugurated a new first for the American army: the firing of a thirteen-gun salute. Clearly, the spirit of independence lived on.

Having marched 140 miles in eleven days in bad weather and without shelter, or adequate clothing and shoes, Washington's army was in sad condition in late September of 1777. But the general showed no signs of discouragement.

Immediately after the Battle of Brandywine, he fired off several orders calling for reinforcements from New York, New Jersey, and Maryland. And on September 26, he moved his main army, which had now grown from 8,000 to 11,000, to a campsite at Pennypacker's Mill on the Perkiomen Creek (now Schwenksville, Pennsylvania).

The same day, Cornwallis took possession of Philadelphia with two Hessian and two Grenadier battalions, two squadrons of Dragoons, and ten guns. The rest of Howe's army camped in Germantown, northeast of the city. It was a tempting target. In a letter to Martha, Washington said, "We are hoping for another Trenton."

At a tense council meeting at the end of September, it was agreed that the army would launch a surprise attack on Germantown from four directions, beginning at 9 P.M. on October 3, only six days after the last of Washington's reinforcements arrived in his camp.

As the sun rose on October 4, so did a fog—a fog so thick it obscured landmarks, distorted sound, and cut visibility to thirty yards. Directly ahead of

Washington's advancing troops, there was an explosion of gunfire as a major battle erupted. The attempt to surprise the enemy had obviously failed.

The fog, combined with the smoke from muskets and artillery, covered the battlefield like a blanket, shrouding it in almost total darkness.

As planned, General Thomas Conway's light infantry had advanced along Germantown Road ahead of Sullivan. Sullivan's column, however, halted when a squad of more than a hundred redcoats fired on it from the upper story of a stone house on the eastern side of the street.

Small cannon were brought up and commenced firing. The building, called the Chew House, was so sturdy, however, that the guns had little effect.

After a precious half-hour delay, the troops skirted the house and continued their advance. Now there was firing from the left. Greene had arrived! Soon the enemy appeared to be falling back on all fronts, leading Washington and his officers to believe that victory was within their grasp.

But, no! On the left there were confused shots, shouts, and more firing. Washington looked in that direction, but could see nothing. Suddenly, however, scores of his own men streamed toward him through the fog and smoke, mouths agape and eyes filled with terror.

"Our men are shooting at each other!" an officer called to Washington.

Spurring his horse among the fleeing men, Washington tried to halt the panic. It was no use. By ten o'clock that morning, the battle was over. The fog had won.

After the Battle of Germantown, Washington led his army twenty-four miles west to Pennypacker's Mill. Since he and his men had covered roughly the same distance the night before and engaged the British in strenuous combat for several hours, all were exhausted.

The next morning, Washington made a report to Congress. The fog, he said, ". . . by concealing from us the true situation of the enemy, obliged us to act with more caution and less expedition than we could have wished, and gave the enemy time to recover from the effects of our first impression; and what was still more unfortunate, it served to keep our different parties in ignorance of each other's movements, and hindering their acting in concert."

The panic among his troops began, he added, when General Stephen disobeyed orders and sent his men to the right and into troops commanded by General Wayne. Blinded by the fog and smoke, the Americans mistook each other for the enemy and opened fire. That, he said, caused the panic and ". . . more than anything else contributed to the misfortune which ensued."

An inquiry revealed that Stephen had been found intoxicated in a fence corner during the battle. The general was subsequently court-martialed, found guilty of drunkenness while on duty, and discharged.

Stephen had been with Washington in the French and Indian War and, when sober, was a competent and brave leader. It was with great sadness that Washington signed the court-martial and discharge papers. On the other hand, he was delighted to give Stephen's command to Lafayette who, with his wound healed, had performed well at Germantown.

Although outmaneuvered at Brandywine and repulsed at Germantown, a new spirit seemed to pervade the army. And in most quarters, Washington's esteem rose considerably. Congress and the public applauded the bold attack on the British, especially since it took place so soon after the retreat from Brandywine.

There were a handful of enemies, both inside and outside Washington's command, however, who soon began plotting to replace him.

And by the time the army went into winter quarters in a place called Valley Forge, Washington was in the most agonizing and perilous situation of his life.

Part Two

In the shape of a rough triangle, the Valley Forge camp grounds were about eighteen miles northwest of Philadelphia. The site gave the American army a good defensive position with plenty of water and wood. There was also an iron-works, a small forge, a sawmill, and a stone house along Valley Creek, which formed one side of the triangle and emptied into the Schuylkill River, a second side. One thing the site did not have was shelter. Nor was there much food or forage to be had in the immediate vicinity.

The army arrived at Valley Forge not long after the Battle of Germantown and the evacuation of its defenses along the Delaware River after a bitter struggle. The retreat gave the British complete control of Philadelphia and easy access to the sea.

It took the tattered American army a week in snowy, frigid weather to travel the thirteen or fourteen miles from its old camp to the new. For three of those days on the frozen, rutted roads, the troops were without bread.

Of this painful march, Washington was to say later, ". . . you might have tracked the army to Valley Forge by the blood of their feet."

Arriving the week before Christmas, the men lived in tents and had to lie on the frozen ground at night, most of them without blankets.

Washington asked the men to build huts for themselves, specifying that each hut should be fourteen by sixteen feet with a chimney and a fireplace, and a roof six and a half feet above the floor. The huts, each of which was to be occupied by twelve men, were to be arranged by regiments in what amounted to small villages connected by rough roads.

Washington said he would "share in the hardship and partake of every inconvenience."

Despite a scarcity of tools, the men went to work felling trees and dragging them to the appropriate building site. Since the soldiers had no nails, the trees had to be notched, fitted together, and sealed with clay.

A few days later, the army ran out of food. In protest, the troops imitated the mournful hoots of owls and the noisy Caw! Caw! of quarreling crows. Later, Washington and his officers heard the men chant dolefully, Nooo Meat! Nooo Meat! Nooo Meat!

When Washington asked the commissary officer when he expected more food, the soldier replied, "I don't."

Washington promptly sent a message to Congress: "Unless some great capital change suddenly takes place . . . this Army must inevitably be reduced to one or the other of these three things. Starve, dissolve, or disperse. . . ."

As he struggled valiantly to hold his army together in the bitter winter of 1777–1778, Washington suddenly faced a new menace—a conspiracy to oust him as commander in chief.

The "cabal," as it came to be called, began to surface when Brigadier Thomas Conway started writing letters to members of Congress and others who were critical of Washington's military ability.

Conway had been among the large group of former French army officers who joined the American forces in 1776. He had a long nose, a small chin, a receding hairline, and eyes that bulged slightly. Those who knew him said he also had "a big mouth," meaning he talked too much.

Although born in Ireland, Conway had extensive training in the French army and saw himself as an expert in military matters. As a result, his letters to prominent individuals, while filled with flowery and indirect language, came to this: Conway knew more about military affairs than anyone else in the Continental Army; Washington's talents as a military commander were "miserable indeed"; and Conway would resign if he didn't get a promotion.

Washington soon learned that there were plans afoot to promote Conway over the heads of twenty-three brigadiers, all of them Conway's senior in length of service. Washington, who had faulted Conway's performance at Germantown, became so angry he wrote to Virginia Congressman Richard Henry Lee, saying, "Conway's merit as an officer, and his importance to this Army, exists more in his imagination than in reality." Promoting Conway, he said, would deliver "a fatal blow to the existence of the Army."

Washington then made this startling statement: "To sum up the whole, I have been a slave to the service; I have undergone more than most men are aware of to harmonize so many discordant parts; but it will be impossible for me to be of any further service if such insuperable difficulties are thrown in my way."

The implication seemed clear: to get rid of Washington, his enemies need only promote Conway.

On a particularly cold day at Valley Forge, Alexander Hamilton peeled back the flap of the Headquarters tent.

"You have a visitor from York, sir," Washington's aide said with a dark look on his face.

A lone visitor from York, where Congress was sitting, to Valley Forge in mid-winter? "Who is it?" a perplexed Washington asked.

Instead of answering, Hamilton stepped aside. Into the tent strode Thomas Conway!

"Well!" a startled Washington exclaimed. "What brings you here?"

"You haven't heard?" Conway asked smugly.

"I have not," Washington answered sharply.

"I'm your new inspector general," Conway said, his smile widening.

"You're my what?" Washington cried out.

"Your new inspector general," Conway repeated.

"I have not heard a word of this from Congress."

"I was appointed by the Board of War," Conway replied, obviously enjoying the situation. "It was thought that matters could be speeded up if I told you of the appointment myself."

"May I see your papers?" Washington said coldly.

"Certainly," Conway said, handing them to Washington.

The papers stated that Conway had indeed been promoted to inspector general. Taking a deep breath, Washington said solemnly, "You realize your promotion will not be happily received by the brigadiers who are your juniors?"

"Perhaps. But it must be realized that I will not be commanding troops. I will be on your staff."

Washington looked at Conway's papers again. "I see you are to take steps to safeguard government property and instruct the troops," he said.

"Correct."

"And has the Board of War given you the set of training instructions you are to follow?" Washington asked.

"Really, General," Conway replied condescendingly, "I don't need training instructions to proceed."

"Perhaps, but you are not to approach my troops without them."

With that, he handed Conway his papers and returned to his work without another word.

Miffed, Conway left.

Washington's internal problems were not limited to Conway.

They escalated in mid-October when General Horatio Gates won the most important victory of the war by defeating General Burgoyne at Saratoga. This victory, in contrast to Washington's defeats, caused many in and out of Congress to support Gates as a replacement for Washington. Among the most vocal was Dr. Benjamin Rush, a signer of the Declaration of Independence.

In a letter to John Adams, Dr. Rush praised Gates's army as "a well-regulated family"; Washington's, he said, could only be compared to "an unformed mob."

Gates, said Rush, was at "the pinnacle of military glory, exulting in the success of schemes planned with wisdom and executed with vigor and bravery."

Washington, on the other hand, was "outgeneraled and twice beaten. . . ." Rush then called for an inquiry into Washington's conduct of the war.

Inevitably, such rumblings reached Washington's Headquarters. For the most part, he shrugged

Although they had once been friends, General Horatio Gates turned against Washington after Gates was given credit for defeating British General John Burgoyne at Saratoga.

them off. But it became increasingly clear that General Gates no longer saw Washington as his commander in chief. For weeks, Gates had been sending his dispatches to Congress instead of to Washington, his commanding officer.

"He thinks we are now two separate commands!" Washington commented bitterly to his staff.

"For the time being," Hamilton said quietly.

Washington said nothing, but he knew what his young aide meant. Buoyed by his victory over Burgoyne and encouraged by his friends in Congress, Gates already saw himself in Washington's shoes.

In early November, Washington received a letter from General Stirling about military events in Reading, Pennsylvania, where he had temporarily set up Headquarters for his troops.

At the end of the letter, Stirling said: "The enclosed was communicated by Colonel Wilkinson [an aide to Gates] to Major McWilliams [Stirling's aide]. Such wicked duplicity of conduct I shall always think it my duty to detect."

The "enclosed" was a single sheet of paper that contained a brief but ominous message: "Heaven has determined to save your country; or a weak General and bad Councellors would have ruined it."

That sentence, Stirling said, was: ". . . In a letter from General Conway to General Gates."

Conway to Gates! Two of his own generals conspiring to discredit him! "Colonel Harrison!" Washington called out.

When Colonel Robert Harrison rushed in, an

agitated Washington said he wanted to dictate two identical notes—one to General Gates and the other to General Conway.

"Yes, sir," a bewildered Harrison said, seating himself with his writing material.

"Sir: A letter I received last night contained the following paragraph," Washington dictated rapidly. "In a letter from General Conway to General Gates he says, 'Heaven has been determined to save your country; or a weak general and bad counsellors would have ruined it.'"

Aghast, Harrison stopped writing. "I didn't think Conway even knew Gates," the astonished secretary said.

"Neither did I," Washington growled.

"Anything else, Excellency?" asked Harrison, a worried frown on his handsome face.

"I think I've said enough," Washington responded as he turned to other matters.

Even during his darkest days, Washington had but one objective: to win the war and get back to Mount Vernon. And while he detested controversy, the discovery that Gates and Conway were part of a loose conspiracy to defame him continued to be irksome.

Both Conway and Gates kept the controversy alive by writing him letters and talking to anyone who would listen. Each, in his own way, offered all sorts of self-serving explanations and protestations about their respective role in the "Conway Cabal." Gates, for instance, said the original communication from Conway that criticized Washington "was harmless" and "a wicked forgery." In a letter from Conway, the new inspector general also insisted he was innocent of any disloyalty. "Therefore, sir," Conway told Washington, "I must depend upon your justice, candor and generosity, for putting an end to this forgery."

While both men offered to make the "forgery" public and send Washington a copy, they never did.

To rid himself of this aggravating situation, Washington simply ignored Conway. As for Gates, he finally sent a letter to his subordinate through Congress, which pointed up many contradictions in Gates's letters—all of which had gone to members of Congress.

General Gates quickly attempted a reconciliation. He said he no longer had any "personal connection" or correspondence with Conway. Then he added: "In regards to the parts of your Excellency's letter addressed particularly to me, I solemnly declare that I am of no faction [conspiracy]; and if any of my letters . . . convey meaning, which . . . is offensive to your Excellency, that was by no means [my] intention." Washington accepted this peace offering, saying the matter would be buried "in oblivion."

While Washington had adroitly put Gates and

Conway in their place, there were still other conspirators sniping at him. But he paid them no mind, primarily because of what happened one night as he walked through the camp at Valley Forge.

Alone and unseen in the darkness, he heard a group of soldiers offer a toast with their meager ration of rum:

"No Washington, no army!"

Washington knew then that the battle with his internal enemies was over.

The battle for American independence and the rights of individuals, however, was not.

Amidst all the internal strife that centered on Valley Forge in the winter of 1777–1778, Washington and the army continued their fight for survival against three principal enemies: disease, starvation, exposure.

Washington's Orders of the Day, mostly written by aides, often clearly revealed what was on the commander's mind. Two days before Christmas, for example, his order read: "Our want of provisions increases and disaffection is beyond belief. Since July we have had no assistance from the Quartermaster General, Major General Thomas Mifflin [a member of the Conway Cabal], whom—to our advantage—resigned in November.

"Soap, vinegar and other articles allowed by the

Washington and his men suffered not only from severe weather at Valley Forge during the winter of 1777-1778, but from disease, a near famine, and lack of clothing and shelter as well. No army in history, Washington said, had endured "such uncommon hardships."

Congress we see none of nor have seen since the Battle of Brandywine. Few men have more than one shirt, many only the fragments of one, and some none at all. A number are confined to hospitals for want of shoes and others in farmers' houses for the same account."

Only 8,000 of the more than 11,000 at Valley Forge were fit for duty, he said. And 4,000 were so poorly clothed they couldn't leave their huts. (By the end of the winter, 2,000 had died.)

The shortage of food was worsening. "The melancholy and alarming truth is," Washington said, "there is not a single hoof of any kind to slaughter and less than twenty-five barrels of flour! We do not know when to expect more."

As he struggled to keep his army together, Washington also bombarded the states and Congress with often emotional letters about the way his troops had to suffer because of the lack of food and supplies. In one letter, he said: "Without arrogance or the smallest deviation from truth it may be said that no history, now extant, can furnish an instance of an army's suffering such uncommon hardships as ours have done and bearing them with the same patience and fortitude. To see men without clothes to cover their nakedness, without blankets to lay on, without shoes—by which their marches may be traced by the blood of their feet—and almost as often without provisions . . . marching through frost and snow, and at Christmas taking up their winter quarters within a day's march of the enemy, without a house or hut to cover them till they could be built . . . in my opinion can be scarce paralleled."

In a letter to Governor William Livingston of

New Jersey on December 31, he spelled out the misery surrounding him with a single sentence: "Our sick naked, our well naked, our unfortunate men in captivity naked!"

In response to Washington's pleas, Congress appointed a committee to review conditions in all departments, particularly the quartermaster general's, which had been under direction of General Mifflin.

Clearly, the committee reported, Mifflin's department had been sorely neglected. "We find the property of the continent dispersed over the whole country," it reported. Wherever the committee looked, it discovered that hundreds of wagons and thousands of tools, tents, and other critical stores had been abandoned or otherwise neglected. The departments for food and clothing (commissary and clothier) were found to be equally in disarray.

Soon afterward, Washington persuaded Nathanael Greene, his best combat general, to accept an assignment as quartermaster general. New heads were also appointed to the commissary and clothier departments. Improvements were noticeable almost immediately.

During February, the army's worst month at Valley Forge, things also improved spiritually for

Washington. Martha was on her way.

It was late afternoon when Martha Washington arrived in Valley Forge. The sun was a pale yellow, the wind stiff out of the northwest, and the temperature far below freezing.

As her chariot rolled and bounced along the rutted road that traversed the heart of the camp, men were working everywhere. With badly chapped hands, cracked lips, and dripping noses, most were carting wood or water. Some were splitting logs. Others were on sentry duty.

One sentry, hunched over against the cold wind with his head, ears, and throat swathed in a big scarf, was standing on his hat to keep his almost bare feet from contacting the frozen ground. When he saw Mrs. Washington, however, he snapped to attention and, with a broad smile, saluted smartly until she passed.

Others, all bearded and unkempt, with rags wound around their feet, hands, and heads, waved vigorously as the chariot passed and croaked out several cheers to "Her Ladyship!"

The sight of the suffering men filled Martha's eyes with tears, but she managed to smile through them and wave back, a small handkerchief wound around her index finger.

Stepping down from the carriage in front of the little farmhouse that was to be her temporary home, she threw herself into her husband's waiting arms and sobbed, "My God, George, why didn't you tell me it was like this?"

She knew the answer, of course; he didn't want her to worry needlessly.

But Martha Washington was not one to give in to despair. Although she was exhausted from the trip and slept late the next morning, it wasn't long before she was involved in a now familiar routine: mending clothes, rolling bandages, helping with the meals, and assisting Washington's aides with the never-ending task of copying orders and letters.

And through it all, she chatted amiably with the aides and the officers who came to call on her husband, asking endless questions about their families and telling anecdotes about her own.

For Washington, Martha was a bright ray of sunshine in an otherwise dismal and discouraging world.

"Friedrich Wilhelm Ludolf Gerhard Augustin, Baron von Steuben."

John Laurens, one of Washington's aides, rolled these names off his tongue with relish as he brought a smartly uniformed foreign officer, along with his aides and a greyhound named Azor, into Washington's Headquarters late in February.

Von Steuben, whose legs seemed too short for his rugged upper body, had a large, fleshy, somewhat comic face. In the middle of his chest, dangling from a bright red, white, and blue ribbon around his neck, was a huge, bejeweled silver star.

Warily, Washington extended a hand in greeting. Another one, he was thinking. "How do you do?" Washington said.

"Wie geht's!" ("How are you?"), von Steuben asked, shaking Washington's hand vigorously.

Washington's face fell. "Doesn't he speak English?" he asked Laurens.

Von Steuben answered for himself. *"Nein!"* ("No!"), he said.

"He speaks French," young Laurens said.

"But not English?"

"Nein!" von Steuben barked again.

Laurens explained that the forty-seven-year-old von Steuben had been a lieutenant general in the king of Prussia's service. He said von Steuben had been recruited by Benjamin Franklin and hoped to serve as an unpaid volunteer.

"But he expects command of a brigade. Correct?"

"No, he thinks that would create problems for you. He would like to observe for awhile, then decide how he might help us."

Turning to von Steuben, Washington said, "Baron, you are most welcome."

"Danke," ("Thanks,") von Steuben said. He saluted briskly and left with Laurens, Azor, and his aides on his heels.

Several days later, Laurens again escorted von

Steuben to Headquarters. "The Baron thinks he can best serve us by instituting a training program for the troops," Laurens told Washington. "With the help of General Greene and Hamilton and me, he believes he can write a manual of arms that will please you."

Washington had heard that the Prussian system of drill and maneuver was superior to that developed by the French and British.

"That would be wonderful," he said. "But how can he teach our men when he can't speak English?"

"There are several of us who speak French," Laurens said. "We can help."

With Washington's approval, von Steuben went to work. Baron von Steuben, with the assistance of Laurens and Hamilton, wrote the American army's first training manual, titled: "Regulations for the Order and Discipline of the Troops of The United States."

Von Steuben began with basics, such as this instruction for a soldier standing at attention when being reviewed:

"He is to stand straight and firm upon his legs with his head turned to the right so far as to bring the left eye over the waistcoat buttons; the heels two inches apart; the toes turned out; the belly drawn in a little, but without constraint; the breast a little projected; the shoulders square to the front and kept back; the hands hanging down at the sides with the palms close to the thighs."

The training methods of Baron von Steuben made a major impact on the Patriot Army. During the siege of Yorktown he commanded three divisions.

Von Steuben also taught the Americans how to fire their muskets in eight counts and—in fifteen counts—to proceed from "Fire" to "Return rammer!"

He developed ten basic commands and learned to give them in English, although with a heavy German accent. Starting at 3 A.M. every day, he drilled one hundred men, hand-picked by Washington and his officers. These, in turn, drilled others.

On April 5, Washington mounted Snowman and, with his aides, senior officers, and a large escort of horse, rode to the perimeter of the Valley Forge encampment to greet a man he had not seen in eighteen months—General Charles Lee.

Lee, who had been captured by the British at Basking Ridge, New Jersey, almost a year and a half earlier, was exchanged for a British prisoner-of-war, Major General Richard Prescott.

When the party of horsemen reached the plateau above Headquarters, they passed by several regiments drawn up on their respective parade grounds. At each location, the regimental fifers and drummers burst into martial tunes.

And thanks to von Steuben's training, the troops, although still in rags, were in perfect alignment as they stood stiffly at attention while Washington's party passed.

Lee was not only followed by his hound dogs that day; he was also followed by the wife of a British army sergeant. This did not go unnoticed by Washington's aides, who entered these few lines to the next day's report from Headquarters:

"A room assigned [Lee] was back of Mrs. Washington's sitting room. When General Lee came out this morning he looked as dirty as if he had been in the street all night. We discovered that he has brought a miserable dirty hussy with him from Philadelphia and actually took her into his room by a back door and she slept with him last night."

In the days that followed, Lee scoffed at von Steuben's training program and offered one of his own titled, "Plan For the Formation Of The American Army in the Least Expensive Manner Possible."

Washington learned later that prior to his arrival, Lee had written to Henry Laurens (the successor to John Hancock as President of Congress and the father of John Laurens, Washington's aide) saying, "I am persuaded (considering how he is surrounded) that he [Washington] cannot do without me."

Washington, desperate for experienced officers, seemed to agree. Those around him were not quite so sure.

Washington always began work long before anyone else was astir in the little Headquarters building at Valley Forge. On April 30, while plodding through the piles of paper, he suddenly realized that this was his third spring as commander in chief.

The end of the war was nowhere in sight. And the problems confronting the army seemed greater than ever. Washington's thoughts that morning were interrupted by the sound of hoofbeats. An express was arriving. A member of the Headquarters Guard still on overnight duty brought him a sheaf of envelopes.

One was from a stranger named Simeon Deane. Curious, he opened it and read the contents—not once, but twice. Then he bellowed: "Martha! John!"

Martha, badly frightened, was the first to arrive at his desk. "What is it, George?" she asked fearfully.

Before he could answer, young John Laurens burst into the room, a pistol in his hand, sure the general was being attacked.

With a joyous smile, Washington held a document aloft and said happily, "France has recognized our independence!"

"It having pleased the Almighty ruler of the Universe propitiously to defend the Cause of the United American-States and finally by raising us up a powerful Friend among the Princes of the Earth to establish our liberty and Independence upon lasting foundations, it becomes us to set apart a day for gratefully acknowledging the divine Goodness and celebrating the important Event which we owe to his divine Interposition."

So wrote Washington in General Orders issued on May 5, 1778. The day "set apart" for the celebration was May 6 and—reflecting the new spirit of the army instilled by von Steuben—began precisely at 9 A.M.

In response to Washington's orders, the brigades, unarmed, were assembled on their respective parade grounds to listen to an open-air reading of the General Orders, the treaty signed with France, and a "discourse" voiced by each chaplain.

One hour later, right on schedule, the ragged regiments loaded their arms and were inspected by their officers. At the single BOOM! of a cannon, the troops smartly formed in two lines in the field, one behind the other.

Now, echoing across the plain and hills came

thirteen more cannon shots. This triggered the most spectacular event of all, a *feu de joie* (fire of joy). Like a string of firecrackers, it began with the firing of thousands of muskets from right to left of front lines and from left to right of back lines.

As the last shot was fired, the jubilant troops shouted in unison, "Long live the King of France." After a few more cheers, and thirteen more cannon shots, the men marched with pride and precision from the field to their quarters and an unexpected reward—a gill of rum.

Near the center of the parade grounds, in a picniclike atmosphere, Washington and Martha entertained the officers and all the wives who were in camp.

Despite the festivities, Washington's mind, as always, remained on duty. From that day on, he said, fatigue parties were excused from work on Sunday and chaplains were to conduct services the same day.

And in one last order, all military prisoners were released, including two soldiers who were to be hanged for desertion.

In the busy days that followed the celebration, there were several developments. With the frost out of the ground, the troops were rapidly burying the disease-bearing dead horses and the trash that littered Valley Forge.

Congress assigned General Gates to the Northern Department, but made it amply clear that he was to be under Washington's orders: General Mifflin was given leave to go to York to defend himself against charges of malfeasance while quartermaster general, and General Lee was given temporary command of General Lincoln's troops (Lincoln had been wounded at Saratoga).

Conway, still complaining about his treatment, offered his resignation. Congress, finally weary of his machinations, accepted. Conway, however, remained in York.

The most startling development of all, however, was this: The British were about to evacuate Philadelphia!

Burgoyne's defeat at Saratoga, combined with the French entry into the war, changed British strategy early in 1778. Sir Henry Clinton replaced General Howe, and the major focus of British effort shifted from the northern to the southern theater.

Thus, toward the end of May, one hundred British ships sailed out of the Delaware River with the enemy's sick and wounded, some three thousand Tories, and much of the army's baggage.

The reason was clear: With the French navy

expected off the coast any day, Clinton couldn't risk putting his troops aboard ship where they could be annihilated by enemy guns.

"He's going overland and traveling light," Washington said. He urged his officers to prepare the army to move at a moment's notice. "When they leave Philadelphia, we must be right on their heels. If they gain a day's march on us, we will have lost a great opportunity to strike what might even be a fatal blow."

On June 16, a teenager known only as Jason was brought into Headquarters by Alexander Hamilton. His mother, he said, washed clothes for some of the British officers.

"Me Mum says you should know the officers give her orders yesterday what was unusual," Jason said.

"Oh?" Washington said. "And what were those orders?"

"She was to deliver all their washin' immediately, 'finished or unfinished.' She said you would know what that means."

Washington did, indeed, know what that cryptic order meant.

Within minutes of Jason's departure, Headquarters buzzed with activity.

Three critical decisions were made:

- General Arnold was to be in charge of a small body of troops that would occupy Philadelphia when the British left.
- Generals Lee and Wayne were to lead six brigades northward as soon as it became clear the enemy had marched out of Philadelphia. These troops were to shadow and harass the enemy.
- Washington would lead the main body on a parallel route to the north, but avoid a total engagement.

At sunrise two days later, General Clinton assembled his army across the Delaware in New Jersey and started north toward Mount Holly.

"March!" was the order that rang across Valley Forge.

Reaching Hopewell, New Jersey, on June 23, Washington held a council of war the next morning. It was a stormy session, with the generals sharply divided on how to proceed.

Lee dominated the arguments, saying it was "absurd" to think the Americans could possibly defeat the British in a head-to-head battle on the plains of New Jersey.

"With the French in the war there is no need to risk a major engagement," he said. "Independence will be ours. All we need to do is wait!"

Knox and Stirling agreed. All the others—especially Lafayette, Greene, and Wayne—pleaded for an immediate and major attack.

When word came that Clinton's army had veered east toward Monmouth Court House (now Freehold, New Jersey), Washington agreed to the plan offered by the trio of dissenting officers. As the senior and most experienced officer, Charles Lee was the natural choice to lead, but he refused the assignment. As a staff officer, Greene could not be considered. Although Stirling was next in line, he was known to occasionally have a problem with alcohol.

Lafayette lacked experience, but this brilliant young officer was courageous and decisive. Washington made up his mind: He ordered Lafayette to take four thousand men to Englishtown, just west of Monmouth Court House, and wait for a good opportunity to strike the British.

Later, when Lee learned of the size of the force, he rushed to Headquarters to object. "Ceding such a command would have an odd appearance," he said and demanded that he be put in charge.

Reluctantly, Washington reversed himself. It proved to be a terrible mistake.

To Washington, Monmouth Court House presented the Americans with their best opportunity to launch a crippling—and maybe fatal—blow to the British army.

To delay meant the enemy could reach the safety of the hills at Middletown, only twelve miles away; and from there it was only another five miles to Raritan Bay and Admiral Howe's ships.

So, in extremely hot weather, Washington led the main body of the American army to Cranbury, another five miles west but would soon move it close to Englishtown, where Lee was now in command of the troops that Lafayette had assembled. On the night of June 26, the commander in chief sent this order to Lee: "Make ready to attack the enemy rear the minute he begins to leave Monmouth Court House."

Back came this strange reply: "From what I know personally of these British officers, they will attack me."

A member of the Headquarters Guard awakened Washington at 5 A.M. on June 28 and handed him a message from Major General Philemon Dickinson, commander in chief of the New Jersey Militia.

"The enemy are in motion [and] making off. . . ." Dickinson, with one thousand militia close to the British advance guard, said his pickets reported that movement from Monmouth Court House began at 4 A.M.

Washington scrambled into his clothes and called Colonel Richard Meade, the officer on duty.

His orders were crisp and precise. "Go to Lee immediately and tell him the enemy is moving and that he is to follow and attack. We will bring the army up to support him as quickly as we can."

As the army got under way toward Lee, Washington sent John Laurens and a new aide, James McHenry, forward on horseback to reconnoiter toward the vicinity of Monmouth Court House.

At that moment, he believed his forces to be positioned as follows:

- Lee was on the enemy's western flank with five thousand men and twelve cannon.
- Big Dan Morgan, a veteran of the French and Indian War who had gone to Quebec with Arnold and had fought at Saratoga, was on the eastern flank with six hundred of his sharpshooters.
- Dickinson was ahead of the British line with one thousand militia.
- Washington's army of 7,800 was moving toward the enemy. Forgetting protocol, Greene was put in command of the right wing, Stirling the left, and Wayne the center.

By noon, the intense heat and lack of water caused several soldiers to drop to the ground in exhaustion. The rest of the army, however, moved steadily on through the choking dust of a narrow sand road.

Suddenly, Washington heard five cannon shots in a row. Strangely, there was no answering fire from either artillery or small arms. As Washington pondered this mystery, Henry Knox galloped toward him from the east.

"Lee's troops seem confused," he called out to Washington. As Washington started to question Knox, a local farmer walked toward him. "They're retreating," he said indignantly.

Lee retreating when he had been ordered to attack? Impossible! "How do you know this?" Washington asked the farmer angrily.

The man pointed to a fifer standing a few yards away. "He told me. He just came from Monmouth."

Washington turned toward the fifer. "Is this true?" He asked.

"Yes, sir. I swear it!"

Angry and upset, Washington cantered Snowman toward the front. He would find out for himself.

Fifty yards . . . a hundred yards—still no sound of firing. But now, coming around a bend in the winding, sandy road, was the answer: Lee's troops were in orderly, but full, retreat!

Washington was stunned. Was this to be another Long Island?

"Take the men into the woods, let them cool off and rest!" he shouted at his aides as he spurred Snowman forward again.

Fifty yards farther on, coming leisurely toward him at the head of a column of troops, was Charles Lee!

"What's the meaning of this?" Washington barked as he and Lee came abreast of each other.

"Sir, sir?" Lee stammered as though he didn't hear correctly.

"Why," Washington grated, "are you retreating?"

"I . . ."

"You received my orders to attack, did you not?"

"Well, uh, yes."

"Then why did you disobey them?"

Lee seemed to recover a bit. "Confusing intelligence," he growled. "I wasn't going to meet the British when I wasn't sure of my situation. Besides, you know I didn't approve of an attack!"

"To hell with your opinion!" Washington shouted. "You asked for and took command. In doing so, you were obligated to obey orders!"

He couldn't argue with Lee any longer. "Hold the men," he shouted as he wheeled Snowman and galloped toward the front.

His aide, Robert Harrison, came hurrying toward him. "The enemy is fifteen minutes away and pressing hard," Harrison called out.

The army had to make a stand. But where?

Lieutenant Colonel David Rhea volunteered that he knew the country. Rhea pointed to the left,

"Yonder is high ground with a swamp in front of it and woods to the rear," he said. "Ideal for a defensive stand."

Washington snapped up this bit of intelligence and immediately ordered Lee's troops to the left. Sure enough, the ground was as Rhea described it.

Now, he thought, we have a chance.

"Bring up more artillery!"

"You, there, off to the right!"

"And you—to the left!"

"Steady in the center!"

By dint of hard riding and a series of crisp commands, Washington somehow managed to get the troops turned around and make a stand behind what was known locally as the West Ravine.

In less than an hour, responding beautifully to their training, the divisions were aligned pretty much as before: Wayne was in the center behind a hedgerow, Stirling was on the left, Greene was on the right, and Lafayette was in a backup position that left him free to move where he might be needed.

Clinton had formed two lines of light infantry, horse, and artillery directly in front of Wayne.

The battle began when Clinton, probing for a weak spot, attacked Stirling and attempted to envelop his left. But the rebels, with encouragement from Stirling, Washington, and von Steuben, shattered the assault in a fierce one-hour exchange of musketry and cannon.

Clinton now ordered troops under Cornwallis to attack Greene on the right. But Greene's men, like Stirling's, splintered the massive enemy assault and drove the redcoats off after a hot fight.

A third attack was directed at Wayne. This one began with a charge of cavalry. As the horsemen galloped toward his position, Wayne shouted, "Steady! Steady! Wait for the word, then pick out the King birds (officers)."

When the cavalry closed to within a few yards, Wayne shouted, "Fire!" Down went horses and men in a bloody heap. Those who survived wheeled their mounts and fled.

Among the fallen was the British leader, Lieutenant Colonel Henry Monckton. He was shot out of the saddle so close to the Americans they were able to capture his body and the battalion's colors.

By late afternoon, Clinton had had enough. His objective now was to disengage and get his army back on the road north.

Washington, however, was determined to deliver a knockout blow. By the time reinforcements arrived, however, it was almost dark and Clinton had withdrawn his troops.

Besides, the oppressive heat and lack of water literally killed scores of men on both sides. It was useless, Washington saw, to try to go on.

During the night, Clinton borrowed a trick

from Washington: His men slipped away while Washington's army slept. Thus ended the battle of Monmouth Court House.

As Washington led his troops to the north and west, he boiled inwardly about Lee's conduct. The eccentric Englishman, he was convinced, had cost his army a major victory. Still, he wasn't sure what action, if any, should be taken.

Lee himself solved the problem with this letter dated June 28, 1778:

"From the knowledge I have of your Excellency's character, I must conclude that nothing but misinformation of some very stupid, or misrepresentation of some very wicked person, could have occasioned your making use of such very singular expressions as you did on my coming up to the ground where you had taken post; they implied that I was guilty either of disobedience of orders, of want of conduct, or want of courage. On which of these three articles do you ground your charge?"

Lee demanded an answer so he could ". . . prepare for my justification, which I have confidence I can do to the Army, to the Congress, to America, and to the world in General."

Lee claimed "the success of the day" at Monmouth was "entirely owing" to his actions and maneuvers. Washington was "guilty of an act of cruel injustice" which gave Lee the right to "demand some reparation for the injury committed. . . ."

Washington coolly replied: "As soon as circumstances permit, you shall have an opportunity either of justifying yourself to the Army, to Congress, to America and to the world in general; or of convincing them that you were guilty of a breach of orders and of misbehavior before the enemy . . . in not attacking them as you had been directed and in making an unnecessary, disorderly and shameful retreat. . . ."

Lee now insisted on an immediate court-martial so his name could be cleared. When Washington read Lee's latest request he ordered his immediate arrest, accusing him of: (1) not attacking the enemy on June 28 as instructed; (2) misbehavior the same day before the enemy and making an unnecessary, disorderly, and shameful retreat; and (3) showing disrespect to the commander in chief in two letters.

When the trial began under General Stirling, witnesses for the prosecution included Alexander Hamilton, John Laurens, and Anthony Wayne. Several witnesses also appeared for Lee. But Lee, who conducted his own defense, failed to cross-examine any of the prosecution witnesses.

Lee was found guilty as charged and given a one-year suspension from the army, a sentence that Congress might or might not approve.

Lee's trial took place on the morning of July 4 in Brunswick. When it was over, the army celebrated not only the verdict but also what it considered a victory at Monmouth and the second anniversary of the Declaration of Independence.

For some, a bit of news from Philadelphia added much joy and merriment to the occasion. Thomas Conway, who lost his job as inspector general and was hanging around Congress hoping for appointment to another post in the army, felt that General John Cadwalader, on duty in the city, had insulted him. He challenged Cadwalader to a duel with pistols. Cadwalader accepted the challenge and chose dawn of July 4 for the confrontation.

When the two wheeled and fired, Conway missed. Cadwalader's ball went through Conway's mouth. "How appropriate," someone at Headquarters said.

While recovering from his near-fatal wound, Conway wrote a final letter to Washington in which he apologized for ". . . having done, written, or said anything disagreeable to your Excellency. . . . You are in my eyes the great and good man," he added.

Washington didn't answer.

When fully recovered, Conway left for France, quickly rejoined the French army, and later served in India and Africa.

In leisurely stages, Washington moved the army northward from Brunswick to the vicinity of White Plains, New York, where he could block the Hudson River, guard the road to Connecticut, and watch Clinton in New York.

From Philadelphia on July 11, General Arnold sent Washington the news he longed to hear: A French fleet under command of Vice Admiral Count d'Estaing was headed for New York!

When he arrived, however, d'Estaing gave up any attempt to attack part of the British fleet inside Sandy Hook because of shallow water. In response to a suggestion by Congress, he sailed for Newport, Rhode Island. The plan, agreed to by Washington, was to have d'Estaing join forces with Sullivan, Greene, and Lafayette in an attempt to capture a key British garrison that had occupied Newport since 1776.

Early in August, the Americans crossed from the mainland to the north end of Newport, an island, and began a push southward.

At virtually the same time, d'Estaing sailed to the western side of the island, but just as he was landing his troops and beginning to bombard the British fortifications, there was a sudden flash of excitement aboard his flagship: Enemy sails were spotted on the southern horizon!

$\mathcal{B}$it by bit, the reports trickling in from Rhode Island gave Washington a picture of what happened at Newport.

D'Estaing challenged thirty-five British men-of-war on the high seas. After maneuvering for two days, both fleets were hit by a severe storm and badly damaged. The French flagship, for example, was dismasted and lost its rudder.

The vessels limped away from the battle scene for refitting and repairs—the French to Boston, the British to New York. Within hours after it became known that d'Estaing was sailing to Boston, Washington learned, there were wholesale desertions among the newly raised divisions of New England militia.

A letter from Greene dated August 31 was more encouraging, however.

"On the evening of the 29th, the Army fell back to the north end of the island," Greene said. "The next morning, the enemy advanced upon us in two columns upon the east and west road. Our light troops, commanded by Colonel Livingston and Colonel Laurens, attacked the heads of columns about seven o'clock in the morning but were beat back; they were reinforced by a regiment upon each road. The enemy still proved too strong.

"General Sullivan formed the army in order of battle, and resolved to wait their approach upon the ground we were encamped on and sent orders to the light troops to fall back."

He said the enemy quickly occupied hills that overlooked the American left and right flanks.

To Washington, the most interesting aspect of the battle at Newport was that a full division of black soldiers, recruited in Rhode Island only weeks earlier with Washington's approval, were in the thick of the battle and helped shatter the three enemy attacks that threatened to crush American forces late in the day.

These soldiers, under Christopher Greene, a white colonel, fought off the tough Hessian regulars they faced with what was described as "desperate valor." Their performance strengthened the convictions of Washington, John Laurens, Nathanael Greene, and others that a strong effort should be made to recruit blacks for the army, especially in the slave-holding states of the South.

Although such an effort failed, some five thousand African Americans served the budding nation in its war for independence, and many gained their freedom from slavery and applied for and were granted pensions.

With Britain and France at each other's throats, the focal point of the war shifted away from the United States to other parts of the world, primarily the West Indies.

There, the two archenemies fought for control

of several islands that were a rich source of sugar and indigo (a plant used for making dye).

This meant that America was locked in a war that was being directed by the heads of government located in London and Versailles. "We are now dancing to someone else's tune," Washington said.

Not strong enough to attack the enemy in New York or Rhode Island, Washington could do nothing but wait until his French ally again turned his attention—and his fleet—to the struggling new nation.

As the months passed, however, Washington wrestled with ways to clothe, feed, arm, and discipline his army. He also had to maintain an ongoing relationship with Congress, thirteen state governments, and his French ally. And he had to referee a long series of disputes over rank and pay among his officers and foreign officers.

"There seems to be no end to my problems," he said in a letter to his brother, Jack.

In November 1778, Washington established Headquarters at Middlebrook (now Bound Brook), New Jersey, and immediately put his troops to work building huts for themselves, just as they had at Valley Forge.

Once the camp was settled, he rode to Philadelphia and met Martha for the Christmas holidays. Still, he was not free from the duties of his command.

Three of his generals had resigned. Two others

gave notice. Then General Lee wrote a newspaper article that aides John Laurens and Alexander Hamilton thought was insulting to the commander in chief.

When Washington heard that Hamilton wanted to duel Lee "to shut his mouth," he told his young aide, "You are not to issue a challenge. And that's an order!"

Laurens was under no such restriction. Determined to retaliate for the perceived attack on Washington's character, young Laurens challenged Lee, and Lee accepted. Alexander Hamilton promptly agreed to act as Laurens's assistant.

After standing back-to-back with pistols raised, the two men, on signal, took fifteen steps forward, turned and fired. Lee missed. Laurens didn't, wounding Lee seriously. Both wanted to try again. "No," Hamilton said. "This has gone far enough." Reluctantly the duelists agreed.

At about this time, Congress finally voted to uphold Lee's conviction, which meant a year's suspension.

Not long after celebrating their twentieth wedding anniversary in January 1779, the Washingtons left Philadelphia and journeyed north to the commander's winter headquarters at Middlebrook.

Benedict Arnold followed a few months later.

When he arrived, he was seated in the cabin of a shiny new phaeton pulled by a pair of smartly harnessed and matched bay geldings.

In a private meeting with Washington, Arnold disclosed that he and Peggy Shippen had been married on April 8. (She was nineteen, he was thirty-eight.)

"Wonderful!" Washington said. "I trust you both will be very happy."

"Thank you, Excellency," Arnold said. "But I must tell you that despite my recent marriage, life has not been all that cheery."

"Oh?" Washington said, suddenly concerned.

Arnold pulled a sheaf of papers from inside his uniform jacket. "Yesterday, I was given these," he said. "They say here that I misused state property."

As Arnold sat rigidly in a chair, his wounded leg stretched out before him, Washington quickly read the papers. He saw that there were eight charges, the most important being the unauthorized use of wagons hired by Pennsylvania officials.

"This looks serious," Washington said.

"Yes, but the charges are false!" Arnold barked.

"And what do you expect me to do?" Washington asked calmly.

"Tell them to drop this . . . this inquisition."

"Ah, but if it were that simple. The State has turned to Congress to settle this matter. If, as you say, you are innocent, you should ask Congress to investigate immediately."

[174]

Reluctantly, Arnold took Washington's advice. And while Congress soon decided to look into the charges, it voted to allow Arnold to retain his post.

In mid-March, however, Arnold turned his command over to Brigadier General James Hogun. In a letter of explanation to Washington, Arnold said, "As soon as my wounds will permit, I shall be happy to take a command in the line of the Army and at all times of rendering my country every service in my power."

Then he fired a salvo at his accusers, saying the investigation of the charges against him would prove his accusers were "unprincipled, malicious scoundrels" who had attacked "an innocent person."

Washington shook his head sadly when he read this. But he looked forward to the day that Arnold would again join him in combat.

That day would never come to pass.

By the spring of 1779, as he struggled to hold the army together, Washington had come to realize that Congress had virtually no power to help him. Only the states could allow the seizure of food for the army; furnish the army with troops and sustain them; raise the money, through taxation, to support the various campaigns; and operate the civil government, which included local police, courts, and judges.

Now, there were thirteen armies and thirteen governments. As a result, the phrase "the United States" started to give way to "the Confederated States." To Washington, this splintering of "the empire" represented a serious danger to all Americans, and he argued repeatedly for a strong central government.

"Our political system may be compared to the mechanism of a clock, and we should derive a lesson from it; for it answers no good purpose to keep the smaller wheels in order if the greater one, which is the support and prime mover of the whole, is neglected." America, he added, was "on the brink of destruction. . . ."

Still, when he heard at the end of May that the British were menacing the Hudson Valley below West Point, he resolutely and promptly issued the usual order: "We march!"

In Washington's day, the Hudson River could be navigated by the largest warships for a distance of 150 miles, a stretch of deep water that almost reached Albany, New York.

In the lower Hudson, at West Point, the river narrowed and made two right-angle turns, leaving square-rigged sailing ships vulnerable to shore batteries, especially those above them in the hills.

Washington felt that the double turns at West Point could be blocked. Early in the war he had called on Colonel Thaddeus Kosciuszko, a Polish-born engineer trained in France, to complete work originally planned by a French engineer named de la Radiere. The defenses were to include a system of redoubts and water batteries and sixty-ton chain booms stretched across the river at two places.

On June 25, before the work was finished, however, General Clinton had easily captured two American forts below West Point. One was at Stony Point, on the western shore of the river, and the other at Verplanck's Point, on the opposite shore. The enemy also seized King's Ferry, an important link between the two—important because it was the closest point to New York City at which the Americans could easily and safely operate barges and keep open lines of east-west commerce and communication.

"Clinton is now only twelve miles south of West Point," Washington said grimly. "If they attack and overcome us there, they may wreck the cause."

After sending Martha home from Middlebrook with armed escorts, Washington hurried the army northward. He arrived at West Point early in June, picked up supplies, moved north several miles and set up Headquarters at New Windsor.

During the rest of June and early July, he made several trips downriver on horseback and got close enough to the two forts to observe what was going on through his glass.

"They don't seem anxious to move on West Point, which puzzles me," he told his staff. "But they have already strengthened both forts considerably."

On June 27, Clinton's main force sailed back to New York, leaving some 1,100 men behind.

"It is clear that they intend to stay," Washington told his staff. And then, in what seemed to be an afterthought, he added, "If we let them."

"Friday, 2 July [1779].—By Gnl. Washington's orders went in with a flag to conduct Mrs. Smith to see her sons. . . .

"Wednesday, July 14.—Moved down the hills in front of Stony Point—took the widow Calhoon and another widow going to the enemy with chickens and greens—drove off 20 head of horned cattle from the enemy's pasture, the property of John Deinke, Saml. Calhoon and Jacob Rose—gave them their property. . . ."

So reads part of a journal kept by Captain Allen McLane of the Pennsylvania Line commanded by General Anthony Wayne, and which was part of Washington's main army. Wayne, with Washington's concurrence, had asked McLane to try to get inside the fort at Stony Point and learn what he could about the enemy's fortifications.

Under a flag of truce, McLane had twice penetrated the enemy's defense dressed as a farmer. He found that the works were incomplete and memorized the weak spots. His information was confirmed by a deserter.

Washington promptly sent Wayne a plan of attack that was to begin at midnight on July 15 and was limited to Stony Point. To be successful, Washington's plan would have to be carried out by eight disciplined, fearless army units that were well coordinated.

And lucky.

Stony Point stuck out into the Hudson from the western shore like a gnarled thumb. The British had constructed two lines of defense on the land side, one behind the other. The fort itself, manned by 625 men, sat atop a 150-foot hill guarded by several batteries. It was, however, only partly enclosed.

While the trenches linking the two semicircular defensive lines were incomplete, all the approaches were water-covered swampland, the water rising and falling with the tides.

After reviewing Washington's plan and making a few adjustments, Wayne collected his force of 1,200 light infantry about five miles below West Point.

The plan of attack was as follows:

- Armed only with bayonets, one column would hit the north end of the semicircular defensive lines.
- Under Wayne, a second column with bayonets would attack the southern end.
- Light Horse troops would ride back and forth in the center, firing their weapons and yelling.
- Ahead of the northern and southern columns, units of twenty men, identified as Forlorn Hopes, were to silence the pickets and knock holes in the defensive lines.
- Advance parties of 150 men were to charge in behind the Forlorn Hopes and be followed by the main body of troops.

The attack began as planned with the north and south units making contact with the enemy at virtually the same time. And even though the men had to wade through water that was sometimes up to their waists, the attack was brilliantly executed. The demonstration by the Light Horse in the center, for example, convinced the British that this was the main body of American troops.

Six companies of redcoats promptly charged down the hill. To the amazement of the British commander, Colonel Johnston, they were cut off and captured.

Wayne suffered a face wound that put him out of action for a short period. But he was at the head of his men when, with gleaming bayonets, they rounded up the survivors. To the surprise and relief of the captives, Wayne passed a stern order: "This is not to be another Paoli."

At about daybreak on the morning of July 16, Captain Benjamin Fishbourne pounded into Headquarters on a lathered horse and handed Washington this note:

"Dear Genl: This fort & Garrison with Coln. Johnston are our's. Our Officers & Men behaved like men who are determined to be free. . . . Yours most Sincerely, Anty Wayne."

With the wind blowing downriver on July 16, Washington believed that he had at least a day to capture Verplanck's Point before General Clinton could bring up reinforcements.

When he arrived at the scene of the battle, he immediately ordered the guns on Stony Point to open up on the objective across the river but soon ran out of long-range projectiles. As the day waned, Washington learned that British reinforcements were on the march to Verplanck's from White Plains.

On leaving Stony Point, Washington destroyed the fort and took along with him fifteen big guns and a huge volume of stores. The loot, which was valued at more than $180,000, was divided among his men.

Of Wayne, Washington wrote: ". . . his conduct, throughout the whole of this arduous enterprise, merits the warmest approbation of Congress. He improved upon the plan recommended by me and executed it in a manner that does signal honor to his judgment and to his bravery."

News of the victory touched off a wild celebration in Philadelphia and other locations, while congratulations poured into Headquarters from several sources.

With Stony Point and Verplanck's soon again in British hands, however, it soon became clear that West Point was more important than ever.

Henry Lee was a twenty-three-year-old Virginian who had graduated from Princeton when he was seventeen. He had joined Washington's army in April 1777 as a captain of a troop of Light Horse Dragoons.

"Light Horse Harry," as he became known, had impressed Washington, particularly with the way he often skirmished with British foraging parties while the army was in winter quarters at Valley Forge. His bravery and resourcefulness also won him the plaudits of Congress and a promotion to major general.

When the young soldier was summoned to Headquarters, Washington explained that Powles Hook (now Jersey City), like Stony Point, looked vulnerable to a surprise attack. He said, however, that he would not risk one unless there was a good chance for success.

He then asked Lee to reconnoiter and evaluate the defenses at Powles Hook, which was on the west side of the Hudson River directly opposite the enemy's main base of operations on Manhattan Island. A week later, when Lee made his report and offered to try to take the fort, Washington told the young commander to proceed with his plan.

Lee's attack plan, a copy of Wayne's at Stony Point, was to start at 12:30 A.M. on April 19. At the appointed hour, however, half of one detachment was missing and so were several officers. The tide was also coming in. Captain Allen McLane had checked ahead, however, and reported that all was quiet behind the enemy lines.

"We will go forward," Lee whispered to his men.

By this time, Lee was three hours behind schedule. Still, his men quickly waded through a marsh in chest-high water and—with only the use of their bayonets—were able to overrun the outer enemy defenses and enter the main works. A cannon and a few muskets went off, but scores of sleepy Hessians and redcoats were quickly rounded up, their hands in the air.

Since every trooper's powder had become wet in crossing the marsh, the situation for the Americans suddenly became dangerous; they had been spotted by British sentries across the river, and, as dawn broke, alarm guns could be heard going off in New York.

"Forget the trophies!" Lee shouted. "Let's leave!"

Despite bad breaks, miscalculations, and mistakes, the raid was highly successful. Like Wayne, Lee received a gold medal from Congress, one of only eight awarded during the Revolution.

As Washington waited to see if the British planned to retaliate for his attacks on Stony Point and Powles Hook, there were several important developments.

Britain's Admiral Marriott Arbuthnot arrived in New York on August 25 with several battleships and transports carrying about five thousand British regulars, while France's Admiral d'Estaing had defeated a British fleet in the West Indies and captured the islands of Grenada and Saint Vincent. Convinced that d'Estaing planned to join Washington in an attack on New York, the British suddenly beefed up defenses in and around the city. The enemy guessed wrong.

D'Estaing took his fleet to Savannah, Georgia. In a joint operation with the Americans, he attempted to take the city, which had been held by the British since the previous December. Despite high hopes, however, the allies suffered a crushing defeat on October 9. D'Estaing was badly wounded during the battle, and General Casimir Pulaski, commander of the American cavalry, was killed.

When General Lincoln and the American forces fell back to Charleston, South Carolina, and the French fleet limped back to the West Indies, it marked the end of the major campaigns for 1779.

In the winter of 1779–1780, winter quarters for the army were again established at Morristown, New Jersey. And although the men set to work immediately building new huts, hundreds were still in tents when the snow began to fly.

While several of his officers took over the tavern he had occupied during the previous winter, Washington set up Headquarters in a large white mansion at the edge of town.

During this second winter in Morristown, the

suffering of the army was far greater even than it had been at Valley Forge.

Baron von Steuben, who was made inspector general on Washington's recommendation after the Battle of Monmouth Court House, was appalled at the condition of the troops. He wrote to a friend: ". . . they exhibited the most shocking picture of misery I have ever seen, scarce a man having the wherewithal to cover his nakedness, and a great number very bad with the itch. . . ."

Washington pleaded with the states for assistance, saying that if provisions were not forthcoming, ". . . there is every appearance the Army will disband in a fortnight. . . ."

But Washington and his army were caught in a vicious circle. The paper money that Congress issued was virtually worthless because the states would not back it up with hard currency, such as silver or gold. As a result, farmers and tradesmen would not accept Continental paper money.

At one point, Washington told a friend that meat and bread had become so scarce his men were forced to eat ". . . every kind of horse food but hay."

Reluctantly, Washington began to use force to get provisions. He did, however, give promissory Continental notes in exchange.

The deplorable conditions, of course, caused scores of soldiers and officers to desert. But even as he struggled to keep the army intact, Washington was confronted with a serious new problem: General Clinton had shipped five thousand soldiers to the South. Their objective, he assumed, was Charleston, a city too weak to defend itself.

Amidst all the concerns and difficulties he faced that winter, however, there was the perennial bright spot—Martha.

After a difficult trip, Martha arrived at camp from Mount Vernon at the end of December. She immediately wanted to hear all the news. Washington, who welcomed this distraction from duty, told her that Lucy Knox, wife of the army's commander of artillery, had not made the trip to camp because she was expecting her fourth child in the spring.

"But, you know," Washington added, "any day now, we may have a new baby right here."

"Who?

When Washington said it was Kitty Greene, General Greene's wife, Martha gasped and shook her head. "That girl is either very courageous or very reckless," she said.

A few days later, New Jersey was hit with a blizzard, the worst anyone remembered. In late January, there was another severe snowstorm. When it ended early one morning, the Washingtons received a note from General Greene, whose headquarters were on the far side of the town. The note read: "It's a boy! His name is Nathanael!"

"I've got to get over there," Martha said.

The deep snow, however, delayed the visit for two more days. On her return, Martha gushed on about the beauty of the baby and the pride of the parents. Then, her eyes filling with tears, she told Washington, "You should have seen the gifts."

"Gifts?" Washington asked, not quite understanding.

"Yes," she said, the tears now streaming down her face, "gifts from those poor men out there in their huts. Toys. Dolls. Even a little rocking horse! All hand-made. Imagine. In this cold! Every morning, Kitty said, there were new ones at the door."

Now Washington's eyes filled with tears.

By the summer of 1780, the War for Independence was in its fifth year. The British had control of the South and had withdrawn all of its troops from New Jersey after clashes with the Americans in and around Springfield.

When less than 1,000 of the more than 14,000 men that Washington had called up reported for duty by mid-July, he again cried out for help. ". . . So much is at stake, so much to be hoped, so much to be lost, that we shall be unexcusable, if we do not employ all our zeal and all our exertion."

Then, from Newport, came a letter Washington had long hoped for.

"I have arrived here with all the submission, all the zeal, and all the veneration I have for your person and for the distinguished talent which you reveal in sustaining a war forever memorable. . . ."

It was signed, "Le Comte de Rochambeau." Rochambeau was the commander of five thousand French troops that landed at Newport on July 10 with eight battleships and several smaller vessels under command of Admiral Chevalier de Ternay.

In a prelude to a struggle between Britain and France for control of the high seas, a flotilla of British warships with five thousand troops aboard soon arrived off Newport, however, and blocked the harbor. The French naval vessels were now imprisoned!

When General Clinton took a large body of troops out of New York City and headed for Newport, it appeared to Washington that Clinton had weakened his own main base of operations. Now, Washington decided, was the time to strike!

Rushing to complete plans to attack the city, he told Congress: "The die is cast, and it remains with the states either to fulfill their engagements, preserve their credit, and support their independence, or to involve us in disgrace and defeat."

The lack of men, wagons, food, and forage, however, hampered his movements as he prepared for what could be a critical battle. He immediately decided that the important left wing would go to Benedict Arnold, the right to Nathanael Greene. The remaining assignments and dispositions were worked out when he finally got the army in motion.

One day toward the end of July, Washington was standing on a rock beside his horse at Stony Point, his right eye glued to his glass as he watched his troops cross the Hudson.

Startled by the sound of a horseshoe striking a stone, he whirled around. There, coming slowly toward him on a weary gray, was a Continental officer, one leg pushed forward at an awkward angle. It was Benedict Arnold.

Washington greeted his old friend warmly. And almost immediately the conversation got around to Washington's battle plan. Several times, however, Arnold said he could not ride a horse for any length of time. "I'm not fit for a field command," Arnold insisted. "What I hope for, what I believe I deserve after what I have suffered, is a stationary post."

Washington chuckled. "A stationary post? You'd die of boredom."

"No, Excellency. I'm serious!"

"But where?"

"West Point," Arnold said, a strange note in his voice.

Washington was puzzled and annoyed. "West Point is unimportant now. What's important is putting my left and right wing under command of my best men."

When Clinton learned about the buildup of Washington's army, he hurried back to New York from Rhode Island, his transports still full of redcoats. Too feeble to carry out an attack against a far superior force, Washington scrapped his plans. The "left wing," which was to be put under Arnold's command, became irrelevant.

On August 3, Washington's orders ended with this line: "Major General Arnold will take command of the garrison at West Point."

Benedict Arnold, Washington's best combat general, turned trai-tor but was detected before any real harm was done.

$\mathcal{I}$n mid-July, without Washington's knowledge or approval, Congress put General Gates in command of the Southern Department. A month later, the hero of Saratoga suffered a horrendous defeat at the hands of Lord Cornwallis near Camden, South Carolina. Almost a thousand Americans were killed and another thousand captured.

In his flight from the enemy, Gates covered 180 miles in a little more than three days. Only then did he pause to report to Congress. Angered by Gates's behavior, Congress removed him from his command and opened an inquiry.

At this stage of the war, the Americans were in their weakest state. The enemy had control of the seas and of Georgia and the Carolinas, and were now poised to strike what might be a critical blow in the North via the Hudson River.

Strangely, the sense of doom created by these setbacks worked somewhat to Washington's advantage. Congress gave him "full power" to coordinate activities with the French and Spanish (who had joined France in the war against England)—anywhere in the world!

Washington promptly wrote to Comte de Guichen, the French commander of the West Indies. Forthright and candid, he said the United States was in serious trouble.

"[It is] . . . without finances, its paper credit sunk and no expedients it can adopt capable of retrieving it; the resources of the country much diminished by a five years' war in which it has made efforts beyond its ability. Clinton with an army of ten thousand regular troops, aided by a considerable body of militia is in possession of one of the capital towns and a large part of the state [New York] . . . a fleet superior to that of our allies, able not only to protect him against any attempts of ours, but to facilitate those he may project against us.

"Lord Cornwallis with seven or eight thousand men in complete possession of two states . . . a third at his mercy and his force daily increasing by an accession of adherents, whom his successes naturally procures him in a country inhabited in great part by emigrants from England and Scotland, who have not been long enough transplanted to exchange their ancient habits and attachments in favor of their new residence."

Finally, he told Guichen that if the allies were to emerge victorious, they must have "an unequivocal naval superiority" in North America. Having said that, he could do nothing but wait and hope.

Early in September, Washington agreed to meet General Rochambeau and Admiral de Ternay in Hartford, Connecticut.

In preparing for the journey, he sent this message to Arnold at his headquarters on the east bank of the Hudson opposite West Point: "I shall be at Peekskill on Sunday evening, on my way to Hartford to meet the French Admiral and General. You will be pleased to send down a guard of a captain and fifty at that time, and direct the quartermaster to endeavor to have a night's forage for about forty horses. You will keep this to yourself, as I want to make my journey a secret."

Washington left his Headquarters at New Bridge, New Jersey, on September 17. After crossing the Hudson at King's Ferry, he had dinner with Benedict Arnold at a house owned by Joshua Hett Smith near the Haverstraw Road.

When they parted, Washington shook Arnold's hand warmly and gave him a friendly clap on the back. "Keep up the good work," he said as he mounted his horse and headed to Hartford.

After almost three days of discussions with his allies about possible combat plans, Washington and his entourage left Hartford for the return trip to New Jersey. "On the way," he told his staff, "I want to stop to see the Arnolds and examine the fortifications at West Point."

On September 24, Washington and his party made an overnight stop at Fishkill. As usual, Washington left the next morning without having breakfast. Among those riding with him that crisp autumn day were Henry Knox, Lafayette, Alexander Hamilton, Major James McHenry, and Captain Samuel Shaw, an aide to Knox.

When the trail took the party close to the east bank of the Hudson, Washington suddenly turned down a path toward the river.

"You're going the wrong way, Excellency!" Hamilton called out from behind.

Washington halted his horse and looked at the group following him. "I want to look at the redoubts near the water," he said.

When he saw the glum looks of his companions, Washington laughed. "I know," he said. "You young men want your breakfast. Or is it that you are anxious to bask in the charms of Mrs. Arnold?"

Sheepish looks caused him to laugh again. "Oh, go on. I'll come later. McHenry, you and Shaw can hurry ahead and let the Arnolds know there's a hungry crowd about to descend on them. But tell Peggy not to wait for me."

McHenry and Shaw happily galloped off. The rest reluctantly remained with Washington.

At about 10:30 A.M., Washington and the others finally rode into the drive of the house that served as headquarters for the garrison at West Point and was also occupied by the Arnolds. The large, rambling structure was owned by a Tory named Beverly Robinson, then living in New York City.

Waiting at the door that morning was Major David Franks, an aide to Arnold. "Good morning, Excellency," Franks said nervously. "I'm sorry, but you just missed General Arnold. He received a call not thirty minutes ago to go across to West Point.

He said to give you his regrets and to tell you he'll be back in an hour."

"Fine. How is the mistress of the house?"

"Actually, Excellency, she is quite ill and has kept to her room. She also sends her regrets."

"I understand," Washington said. Then, he asked for Lieutenant Colonel Richard Varick, another Arnold aide.

Embarrassed, Franks said Varick was also ill and confined to his bed.

"Oh, well," Washington said, "we'll have some breakfast. And then we'll cross to the west side and catch up with General Arnold."

Relieved, Franks led the way into the house.

As he was being rowed across the river later that morning, Washington scanned the rocky precipice in front of him. West Point, he saw with pride, was a marvel of military engineering. Gun placements, at high and low levels, were well situated for command of the river. Most of the heavy cannon were trained at a spot downriver where sailing ships would have to make a difficult and slow turn. At that point, too, a huge chain stretched from bank to bank just below the surface of the water.

"There, gentlemen," Washington said with satisfaction," is the greatest fortress in America."

When the party left the barge, no one was in

sight. As it began to climb up the rocky trail, however, Colonel John Lamb, the commandant, came scrambling downhill toward them.

"Good morning Excellency," Lamb puffed as they drew together.

"Good morning," Washington said calmly. "Have you seen General Arnold?"

"No sir, I have not," came the reply.

Despite his concern, Washington continued his inspection of the fort. As he moved along, he began to notice things that alarmed him. Many of the redoubts were weak and in poor condition. And there was dirt and debris everywhere.

Something, he thought, is very wrong.

Hamilton, who had remained at the Robinson house, opened the door when Washington returned at 3:30 P.M. expecting to have dinner at four o'clock.

"Did he come back?" was Washington's first question.

"No sir," Hamilton answered. "And no word from him."

"Mrs. Arnold?"

"She's still indisposed," was Hamilton's reply.

Washington sighed. "Well," he said, "let's get ready for dinner. I suppose there's some explanation for all this."

As Washington was freshening up in his room, there was a knock on his door. It was Hamilton, a bundle of papers in his hands.

"For you, sir," he said. "Sent by a Lieutenant Colonel John Jameson of the First Dragoons."

Washington took the bundle, opened it, and began to read. As he did so, Hamilton left and started down the hall toward his own room. Just as he passed Lafayette's door, he heard an anguished bellow behind him. Hamilton threw open the door to Lafayette's room and yelled, "Come quick, it's the general!"

Both men rushed to Washington's room and burst in. Washington, with a stricken look on his face, said in a voice shaking with anger, "Arnold has betrayed us!"

Recovering quickly, Washington told his aides that the papers included a pass through the American lines for a John Anderson.

"The pass is dated September 22 and signed by Arnold," he noted. "According to the covering note from Lieutenant Colonel Jameson, this Anderson was caught behind our lines on the road for New York.

"When he was searched, they found several papers in his boots beneath his stockings. The papers give a complete description of the defenses of West Point!"

The papers also contained the minutes of a council of war held on September 6, plus the disposition of artillery at West Point. "All in Arnold's handwriting!" he emphasized.

"Who is this man Anderson?" Lafayette asked.

"Jameson says Anderson is really Major John André, an adjutant in the enemy's army," Washington said.

Washington pulled another paper from the packet. "Here," he said, "is a letter from this André. He says he came ashore from the *Vulture* and was to meet someone for some intelligence. Contrary to his agreement, he was taken behind our lines and was forced to put on civilian clothes. Then, he says, he was abandoned and forced to get to New York by land. That's how he was caught."

Washington then read the rest of the Anderson-André letter: "Thus, I have the honor to relate was I betrayed (being Adjutant General of the British Army) into the vile condition of an enemy in disguise within your posts."

"He's a spy!" Hamilton burst out.

"Yes," Washington said grimly. "He is."

Arnold's treachery touched off a barrage of questions among Washington, Hamilton, and Lafayette as they paced about Washington's room that historic afternoon in 1780.

Where was Arnold? How did he escape? Who alerted him to danger? Who else was involved in the plot to give away America's military secrets? Were the British, at that very hour, planning to sail up the river and attack the fort?

Obviously, decisions had to be made. And quickly.

"We will say nothing about what we know until we find answers to some important questions," Washington told his aides.

Washington believed that Arnold had gone downriver to board the *Vulture*. "Get McHenry," he told Hamilton. "Ride to King's Ferry as fast as you can. Maybe you can catch up to his barge before he passes."

Just after Hamilton rushed off, there was a knock at the door. It was a short, pudgy officer with bleary eyes and feverish cheeks. "I'm Varick, sir," the obviously distraught officer said.

"Good afternoon, Colonel," Washington said with a calmness he didn't feel. "Feeling better?"

"A little," Arnold's aide said. "Excellency, Mrs. Arnold is . . . well, she seems to be out of her mind. She just babbles and babbles!"

"About what?" Washington asked.

"Her husband! Over and over, she says 'He's gone forever!' Now she's calling for you, Excellency. She says she has a hot iron pressed against her head and she wants you to take it away!"

The three men found Peggy pacing wildly about

her bedroom, tears streaming down her face and sobbing loudly. Her hair was disheveled, and her scanty night dress hung off one of her shoulders in disarray. In a crib nearby, a baby squalled at the top of its lungs.

Varick, who had entered the room first, said, "Mrs. Arnold. Mrs. Arnold! Here is General Washington. He's come to help you."

The weeping woman stopped her pacing. She took one look at Washington, snatched up the baby, and screamed, "That's not General Washington! That's somebody else. And he's come to kill my baby! Oh, God! Oh, God!"

"Now, now," Washington said soothingly.

Peggy backed hurriedly away to the farthest corner of the room. "No! No!" the panic-sticken woman screamed. "Go away! Go away!"

Realizing the situation was hopeless, Washington left the room with Lafayette and Varick following.

In the hours and days after Arnold's escape, there were several swift, dramatic developments. Washington told Arnold's two aides, Franks and Varick, that they were under arrest until the completion of an investigation. Their private papers, along with Arnold's, were seized.

It appeared that Arnold had deliberately weakened the garrison to leave it vulnerable to an enemy attack. He had, it was learned, sent two hundred men off the post to cut wood and others to assignments elsewhere. The men were recalled, the post put on full alert, and General Greene, in charge of the main camp in New Jersey, was ordered to send a division to King's Ferry immediately.

The *Vulture* sailed with Arnold aboard. Before it left, Arnold sent two letters ashore to Hamilton under a flag of truce. One was to his wife, which Washington sent to Peggy unopened. The other was to Washington. The first paragraph read:

"The heart which is conscious of its own rectitude, cannot attempt to palliate a step which the world may censure as wrong; I have ever acted from a principle of love to my country, since the commencement of the present unhappy contest between Great Britain and the Colonies; the same principle of love to my country actuates my present conduct, however it may appear inconsistent to the world, who very seldom judge right of any man's actions. . . ."

Arnold added that his wife was "innocent as an angel" and asked that she be permitted to return to her friends and family in Philadelphia. He also absolved Franks, Varick, and a civilian, Joshua Smith, of complicity in his treachery.

Peggy Arnold, calmer now after her panic, was allowed to return to Philadelphia the next day. Colonel Jameson was ordered to send Major André to West Point.

Everything was gradually being sorted out and brought under control. Arnold, it became clear, had been acting alone. Still, Washington faced a serious problem: What should he do about André?

André was brought to the Robinson house by Major Benjamin Tallmadge and a strong force of Dragoons. When he arrived after an all-night ride in the rain, he looked like anything but a British officer.

Unshaven and shabby, he wore a round beaver hat, a worn, reddish, nonmilitary coat, common breeches, and a waistcoat. There was, however, one item that gave his costume away: a pair of handsome military boots with white tops.

It was Tallmadge who finally furnished the last piece to the puzzle of how André was captured and Arnold escaped. André, he said, left the *Vulture* and met Arnold on the west shore of the Hudson. When he was about to return to the ship the following morning, an American militia unit fired on the *Vulture* from the east bank with two cannons, driving the vessel downstream. André later crossed the Hudson at Stony Point and started south on the east bank.

"Three militia men—John Paulding, Isaac Van Wart, and David Williams—stopped André on the

Major John André was Benedict Arnold's contact with the British high command. Since he autographed this painting, it apparently was a good likeness.

Old Post Road near Tarrytown," Tallmadge explained to the General. "He was alone and riding to New York. But the way he talked made them suspicious, so they made him dismount and searched him. That's when they found the papers."

"And what happened next?" Washington asked.

"Well, when the prisoner was taken to our outpost, Colonel Jameson decided the papers were forged and sent the prisoner to Arnold with them."

"What?" Washington roared.

"I know, sir!" Tallmadge pleaded. "But, well, me and the colonel had quite an argument. Finally, he agreed to recall Arnold and the papers. But since this John Anderson had a pass signed by Arnold, he insisted on letting General Arnold know John Anderson had been captured. Later, when he heard you were coming, he sent the papers to you."

"How wise," Washington said sarcastically.

Toward the end of the month, Washington received a letter from his enemy, General Henry Clinton. Clinton argued that, since André had gone ashore from the *Vulture* under a flag of truce from Arnold, he was not a spy.

"I have no doubt but your Excellency will immediately direct that this officer have permission to return to my orders at New York."

Washington set the letter aside and named fourteen officers to try André and report ". . . a precise state of his case, together with [their opinion] of the light in which he ought to be considered and the punishment that ought to be inflicted."

After a one-day hearing, the Board of Inquiry, chaired by General Greene, sent Washington this

Sir Henry Clinton replaced William Howe as British commander in chief when France became an American ally.

report: "The Board having considered the letter from His Excellency General Washington respecting Major André, Adjutant General to the British army, the confession of Major André, and the papers produced to them, report to His Excellency, the commander in chief, the following facts, which appear to them relative to Major André.

"First, that he came on shore from the *Vulture* sloop of war, in the night of the twenty-first of September . . . on an interview with General Arnold in a private and secret manner.

"Secondly, that he changed his dress within our lines, and under a feigned name, and in a disguised habit, passed our works at Stony and Verplanck's Points, on the evening of the twenty-second of September . . . and was taken the morning of the twenty-third of September at Tarry Town, in a disguised habit, being then on his way to New York, and when taken, he had in his possession several papers, which contained intelligence for the enemy. . . ." The Board declared that André was "a spy" and "ought to suffer death."

Washington answered Clinton's letter by sending him a copy of the Board's decision. And on October 1, he issued this order: "Major André is to be executed tomorrow at twelve o'clock precisely. . . ."

Instead of being shot as he requested, André, wearing his full uniform, was hanged, the usual punishment for spies.

Only hours after André's death, Washington received another message from Arnold, who was still aboard the *Vulture*. Arnold thought he could persuade Washington to spare André's life. Even if the letter had arrived on time, it would have been a futile attempt; futile because it was more of a threat than a plea for mercy.

If André were executed, Arnold said he would think himself ". . . bound by every tie of duty and honor to retaliate on such unhappy persons of your army as may fall within my power." Then he added: "I call Heaven and earth to witness that your Excellency will be justly answerable for the torrent of blood that may be spilt in consequence."

While Washington ignored the threat, it caused him to write, "There are no terms that can describe the baseness of his [Arnold's] heart."

Publicly, he said, "In no instance since the commencement of the war, has the interposition of Providence appeared more conspicuous than in the rescue of the post and garrison of West Point from Arnold's villainous perfidy."

He now hoped to put the André-Arnold affair behind him. But he was in for a surprise. General Clinton, well aware of Arnold's ability as a combat general, soon put him in a British uniform.

For the fifth consecutive year, Martha Washington made the dangerous and arduous journey to her husband's winter Headquarters, now at New Windsor, arriving before Christmas. Her new home was perched on a hill with a wonderful view of the Hudson River and the opposite shore.

Christmas dinner that year was the best since the war began. While a band played, Washington and his small family of officers and their wives feasted on three turkeys, a cut of beef, some lamb, and lots of apples, nuts, and pudding.

A week later, the warmth of Christmas faded. Anthony Wayne sent word from Morristown that the Pennsylvania line had mutinied and was marching on Philadelphia. Congress had been asked to leave the city.

Luckily, the mutineers ended their march in Princeton and returned to Morristown after negotiations with Pennsylvania authorities who had been rushed to the scene.

Washington, however, was not entirely pleased with the outcome. "When civil authorities intervene in military matters, discipline is lost," he said. "The agreement reached is badly flawed and will have an ill effect on the Army should we face such a crisis again."

The "crisis" came sooner than expected.

On January 21, 1781, Colonel Israel Shreve notified Washington that some two hundred mutineers of the New Jersey Line were marching on Trenton, seat of the state government.

This time, Washington said, there would be no negotiations between the army and civil authorities. He alerted General John Sullivan, telling him to keep members of Congress away from the mutineers to prevent their intervention. Washington planned to put down the rebellion with six hundred hand-picked men. "Unless this dangerous spirit can be suppressed by force, there is an end to all subordination in the Army, and indeed to the Army itself," he said.

Learning that the two hundred mutineers had returned to their huts, troops from West Point under Major Robert Howe surrounded the area at midnight on January 26. On instructions from Washington, Howe's men trained their guns and cannon at the huts.

"You have five minutes to come out!" Howe shouted to the defiant Jersey soldiers.

When all were assembled, Howe asked their officers to identify the ringleaders. Three were named, separated from the group, tried on the spot, and found guilty. On further testimony, one was reprieved; his case was to be reviewed later by Washington.

Howe now asked for the names of those who had followed and supported the ringleaders. Twelve more men were separated from the group.

"Go into your huts and come back with your weapons," Howe told the twelve.

Divided into squads of six each, they were

ordered to execute the two ringleaders who were now on their knees, hands tied behind their backs.

Would they do it? Despite screams for mercy from the doomed pair, they did.

That was the end of the mutiny.

The mutiny of the New Jersey Line early in 1781 had barely ended when Washington learned that 1,600 redcoats were put ashore at the mouth of Virginia's James River.

With his officers gathered around his desk, Washington informed them the enemy had moved to Westham, Virginia, where it destroyed a gunpowder factory and an iron foundry.

"Later, they marched to Richmond, took the town without firing a shot, burned several buildings, and returned to Portsmouth to establish camp," he added. The British, he noted, already had large forces located in Charleston, Savannah, and Camden.

"The troops on the James River can now cut off Greene's communications and supply route from the north."

"He'll soon be in a trap!" Hamilton exclaimed.

"Yes," Washington said gravely. "And unless the French navy gets here quickly, that trap will close and Greene will be destroyed. The British will then have almost complete control of the South."

"Do we know who's in command of the redcoats on the James?" someone asked.

Washington looked around at the faces of his men. "Yes," he said, his eyes flashing angrily, "Benedict Arnold!"

In February 1781, Washington heard from Rochambeau at Newport, Rhode Island, that a massive storm had crippled the British fleet anchored off Gardiner's Island, a small island northwest of the tip of Long Island.

Believing that the French navy was now strong enough to leave Newport, Rhode Island, Washington wrote to Rochambeau asking for full naval support in Virginia from Admiral Charles Destouches.

Because of low funds, Congress had cut back on payments for expresses (faster mail deliveries), and Washington did not receive a response from Rochambeau until February 14.

"I am going at this moment aboard of the Admiral to know whether he intends going out with all his ships, or at least send a detachment of some of them to Chesapeake Bay," Rochambeau had written eleven days earlier. "It is generally looked on as dangerous to go and attack the British in the Bay whose entry is much straiter than it is marked on the maps. But I think two men-of-war and two frigates will destroy all the expedition of Arnold's in Chesapeake Bay. . . ."

Now, Washington ordered Lafayette to immediately march to Virginia with 1,200 men and be ready to join Detouches's squadron at Portsmouth for a singular purpose: Arnold, he said, must be stopped, captured, hanged!

The damage reported to have been sustained by the British fleet off Gardiner's Island was exaggerated. The enemy's navy was still superior to the French. As a result, Destouches chose to order a quick strike at Portsmouth, Virginia, with only a forty-gun warship and two frigates under Arnaud de Tilly.

Washington was deeply disappointed. But, he felt, if de Tilly could keep Arnold bottled up in Portsmouth and prevent him from being reinforced, the French-American allies might have a chance to destroy the traitor with a concerted attack.

Before long, Rochambeau reported that de Tilly had captured the *Romulus,* a British frigate, as well as six other vessels and had taken five hundred prisoners.

In a second message, Rochambeau said: "The letters found on board the vessels taken by M. de Tilly have decided M. Destouches to follow in full the plan given by your Excellency, and to risk everything to hinder Arnold from establishing himself in Portsmouth in Virginia. M. Destouches is arming with the greatest diligence the forty-four-gun ship that was taken, and he hopes this, with the frigates, will be able to go up Elizabeth River. He will protect this expedition with his whole fleet. Your Excellency has given me orders to join thereto one-thousand men. I will send one-thousand-twenty. . . ."

Ironically, at virtually the same moment, Washington learned of a development with far different implications: General Greene was about to withdraw from North Carolina!

Washington was quick to respond. In orders to Lafayette, he said that when the French fleet arrived in Virginia, Lafayette would be free ". . . to concert a plan . . . for a descent into North Carolina, to cut off the detachment of the enemy which had ascended Cape Fear River, intercept if possible Cornwallis and relieve General Greene and the Southern States."

Now, Washington decided, it was time to once again have a personal meeting with the French, this time at their headquarters in Newport, a meeting that would develop a grand plan to end the war!

Washington's first meeting with the top French command took place aboard Destouches's flagship *Duc de Bourgogne*, a huge vessel that carried eighty guns.

A few days later, with plans made and agreed to, Destouches sailed out of Newport. Unfortunately, the British learned of his departure and left Gardiner's Island to meet him on the high seas.

There was a great naval battle on March 16, and while the French could be said to have won it, Destouches felt that Britain's Admiral Arbuthnot, with faster ships, could get to the Chesapeake ahead of him. He returned to Newport.

On May 6, however, the French frigate *Concorde* arrived in Newport. Among its passengers was Comte de Barras, who was to succeed Admiral Destouches. Would Washington care to meet with de Barras and General Rochambeau? Yes!, Washington quickly replied.

The meeting was held at Wethersfield, Connecticut, on May 22. But because British sails were sighted off Newport, de Barras did not attend.

During the meeting, Rochambeau told Washington of a stunning development. "A large French fleet under Comte de Grasse left France with reinforcements," he said. "Part of that fleet, as well as troops, are to go to Newport. De Grasse will remain in the West Indies but may join us later."

The principal question to be decided was this: Should the allies proceed against the enemy's main base in Manhattan, or should they launch their campaign in Virginia?

When Washington was told that de Barras was opposed to ferrying troops to the Chesapeake, he promptly said he favored an attack on New York. "With a move against New York, Clinton will have to withdraw his men from Virginia," Washington pointed out. "That will give Greene and Lafayette the opportunity to take the initiative in that quarter."

He further argued that if de Grasse could be persuaded to leave the West Indies and sail for New York, he might be able to bottle up the British fleet in the harbor. In general, there was agreement to these broad, but loose, plans.

On returning to Headquarters, Washington wrote Lafayette to tell him of the concerted French-American plan to attack New York. Because there were no expresses available, Washington put his letter in the regular mail.

Lafayette never received the letter. It fell into the hands of Sir Henry Clinton.

By the summer of 1781, the six-year struggle to achieve American independence seemed headed toward a climax. These were the developments:

- Clinton sent Major General William Phillips to Virginia with 2,600 men to supplement Benedict Arnold's force and take command. Miffed at being outranked, Arnold returned to Clinton.
- Hoping that de Grasse would bring the French fleet from the West Indies to New York, Rochambeau and Washington had their forces in place on the outskirts of the city.

The immediate objective was to keep Clinton from sending any more reinforcements to Cornwallis in Virginia.

- De Barras and his small fleet were in Newport, held there by the superior power of British warships.
- Cornwallis, campaigning in Virginia, received a letter from Clinton saying, "I beg leave to recommend it to you . . . to take a defensive station in any healthy situation you choose, be it at Williamsburg or Yorktown." And when that position was established, Clinton ordered, Cornwallis was to "immediately embark" three thousand troops northward to help Clinton keep his hold on New York City. In response, Cornwallis concentrated the bulk of his troops on the Virginia peninsula of Yorktown, confident that the British navy would come to his aid, if necessary.
- Lafayette, reinforced by the Pennsylvania Line under Anthony Wayne, faced Cornwallis and was committed to keeping him pinned against the sea. By the same token, Greene was farther south in a position that forced the British to stay where they were in their various strongholds.

On August 14, Washington summoned his top command to Headquarters. Standing behind his desk with the officers seated quietly and expectantly around him, Washington said, "Gentlemen, I have great news. Admiral de Grasse will be coming to the Chesapeake instead of New York. He will have twenty-nine ships and three thousand men. And he will remain until October 15."

Whooping and applauding with joy, the officers jumped to their feet as one man, scattering chairs noisily behind them, for it was now clear that a combined allied land and sea force could trap and destroy Cornwallis and free the South. And in that lucky event, the allies could then concentrate on Clinton and, it was hoped, bring the war to an end. There were, however, two major problems: (1) could de Grasse reach the Cheseapeake before the British navy learned of his plans? and (2) how—in the short period of two months—could Clinton be held in New York while the bulk of the American and French armies moved unmolested to Virginia to attack Cornwallis?

Since the timetable for long sea voyages by sailing ships depended on such variables as the wind, weather, and tides, no one knew the answer to the first question.

There was, however, an answer to the second: Clinton would have to be tricked.

Racing against time, Washington and Rochambeau took a number of critical steps. With the aid of Patriot spies, they let it be known that de Grasse was headed toward New York, and that French troops intended for Virginia would be moved to New Jersey and be prepared to attack Staten Island as soon as de Grasse arrived.

To implement the supposed attack, the Americans gathered up all the boats and pontoons available between Newark and Amboy, and also had an oven designed to bake French bread built in Chatham, indicating that the French planned to stay in New Jersey for a long time.

Only five days after Washington received word about de Grasse's anticipated arrival, he began his march south from the Hudson with three fast-moving columns.

When he reached Springfield, New Jersey, he learned that Clinton had rushed reinforcements to Staten Island. (Washington's intercepted letter to Lafayette helped convince Clinton that an attack was imminent in that quarter.)

"So far, so good," Washington said of his elaborate ruse.

Instead of wheeling toward Staten Island, however, Washington went straight on. Would this fakery continue to work?

On August 27, Washington wrote the governor of Maryland: "The moment is critical, the opportunity precious, the prospects most happily favorable."

Washington reached Trenton on September 1 only to learn that seven ships of the line under Admiral Thomas Graves, plus fifteen battleships, two frigates, and a sloop under Admiral Samuel Hood, had left New York and were steering south. Obviously, the British had been alerted to de Grasse's departure from the West Indies.

The next day, Washington rushed a letter to Lafayette, saying: ". . . I am distressed beyond expression to know what is become of the Count de Grasse and for fear the English fleet, by occupying the Chesapeake . . . should frustrate all our flattering prospects in that quarter. . . ."

Three miles south of Chester, Pennsylvania, Washington was relieved by a dispatch handed to him by a rider astride a lathered horse: De Grasse had won the race to the Chesapeake! Cornwallis was trapped!

In accordance with plans established weeks earlier, the American and French armies marched to Head of Elk during the heat of late August, arriving there early in September. From Head of Elk, the troops, siege guns, and supplies were to travel down the Chesapeake to Virginia aboard a flotilla of boats, which were supposed to be ready and waiting. When Washington reached the boarding area, however, there was only enough shipping available to carry two thousand men!

"Search the shoreline," Washington barked at his officers. "Bring in fishing boats, oyster boats, anything that will float. The wind is in our favor, so hurry!"

As each available boat was loaded with guns, men, and supplies, it was sent on its way. Those men who were left behind followed Washington to Baltimore, where the rest of the needed shipping was found and boarded for the trip south.

Early on September 9, with only one member of his staff at his side, Washington set off on another leg of this historic journey. His destination? Mount Vernon.

Late one night toward the end of August, an express rider brought a letter, marked urgent, from the General to Mount Vernon.

Sending the rider to the kitchen for food and refreshments, Martha ripped open the envelope and glanced at the contents. "He's coming!" she shrieked at the silent house.

From that moment on, Mount Vernon buzzed with activity. To the general's cousin, Lund Washington, Martha said, "Whatever isn't finished must be finished by the time he gets here. Do you realize he's never seen the banquet room, the library, or the new bedroom above? It's been six years, Lund. No. Six years and four months! And he's bringing guests. French guests. He'll want to be proud of us. Of this house. His gardens. The barn. Everything! So hurry, do what you have to do, but get it done!"

To Jacky and Nelly she wrote: "Don't forget, he's never seen your babies! Won't it be a wonderful moment when Little Washington takes hold of his finger, bounces on his lap and laughs that cute little laugh of his? I'll let you know when he's here. And when I send for you, you come!"

When he arrived on September 9, it was dark. But she had heard the thrumming of the horse's hooves on the drive and when he dismounted, she was there, holding the door wide open, a radiant smile on her face. They hugged and kissed without a word. He was home.

When Jacky and Nelly Custis arrived with their four children, Washington broke away from army business to greet them all and, as Martha anticipated, he played joyously with the baby, making all kinds of what Martha called "baby talk."

During this interlude, Jacky made an astonishing request. "I'd like to go with you to Yorktown," he told Washington.

To Martha and Nelly's disapproval, Washington laughed and said, "I suppose you could go along as a volunteer aide."

When it was all settled, Martha and Nelly went scurrying in the attic to find something resembling a uniform for Jacky. They came down with a dark blue coat and a white waistcoat, plus a green sash. The sash, Martha explained, could be worn diagonally across the waistcoat to show he was a personal aide to the general.

After a precious three nights and two days at Mount Vernon, Washington began the long trek to Williamsburg. Less than halfway, however, he received ominous news: De Grasse had left the Chesapeake and disappeared!

A**rriving in Williamsburg a few days later, Washington had a happy reunion with Lafayette and Anthony Wayne. After an elaborate review of the French and American troops gathered there, he became immersed in a series of meetings to plan the siege of Yorktown; a siege—if successful—that might end the war.

On the morning of September 15, Washington was relieved to hear that de Grasse was back. He had sailed out to attack a British squadron, beaten it, and returned with two captured frigates. Even more encouraging was the news that de Barras, with siege guns and a load of salted food, had joined de Grasse.

It was twelve miles from the position of the allies on York Peninsula to the enemy lines. And while the main force remained on the south bank of the York River, a large body of militia, French marines, and French regulars under Marquis de Choisy crossed to the north bank to hem in the enemy on Gloucester Point.

The command "March!" rang out in the various allied camps at sunrise on September 28. For the first time since the war began, Washington realized with satisfaction, he was in command of a superior force. But the battle had yet to be won.

With the French lines stretched to the left and the Americans to the right, preparations for the formal siege of Yorktown began on October 6.

Favored by a dark rainy night, a 2,000-yard-long trench was quickly staked out by the engineers. Some 1,500 men dug all night into the sandy soil and by daybreak had completed their trench and four redoubts.

Washington cautioned his men not to be too eager. "Waste no ammunition," he said repeatedly.

Work continued until there were six redoubts in the first trench. On October 9, the heavy artillery was brought forward. That afternoon, in bright sunshine, the first battery was ready to open fire. On Washington's orders, that honor went to a French officer, the Marquis de Saint-Simon.

By the following day, at least forty-six guns were hammering at the British position. Forward movement, however, was obstructed by two advance British redoubts some six to seven hundred yards in front of the Americans.

The French engineers solved this difficult prob-

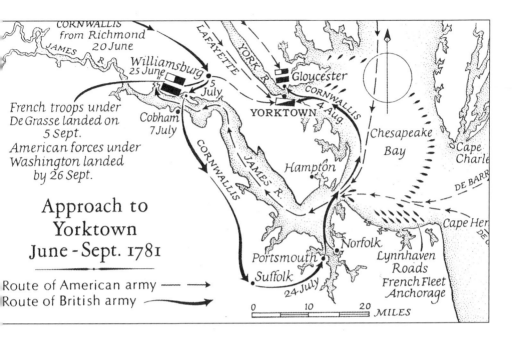

French troops under
De Grasse landed on
5 Sept.
American forces under
Washington landed
by 26 Sept.

**Approach to
Yorktown
June - Sept. 1781**

Route of American army — →
Route of British army —

*CORNWALLIS
from Richmond
20 June*

JAMES R.

*Williamsburg
25 June*

*5
July*

*Cobham
7 July*

LAFAYETTE

YORK R.

Gloucester

CORNWALLIS

YORKTOWN

4 Aug

*Chesapeake
Bay*

*Cape
Charl*

CORNWALLIS

JAMES R.

Hampton

DE BARR

DE

Cape Her

Norfolk

Portsmouth

*Lynnhaven
Roads*

*French Fleet
Anchorage*

Suffolk

24 July

0   10   20
MILES

lem by building an *epaulement,* a trenchlike construction to the right of the British redoubts. Now, the two troublesome redoubts were vulnerable to a direct assault.

At dawn on October 14, the allies began firing at the outer redoubts to soften them up. At two o'clock, word was passed that the French would storm the left redoubt and the Americans, under Lafayette, would storm the right. Lafayette chose his aide, a Frenchman named Jean-Joseph Sourbader de Gimat, to lead the charge. Hamilton objected. "I have seniority and since I do, I'm entitled to command," he protested. Asked to settle the dispute, Washington sided with Hamilton.

Firing ceased as night came on. At seven o'clock a signal shot was fired. Out charged the Americans and Frenchmen. Within an hour, both redoubts had fallen.

The French-American fighters moved closer and closer to Cornwallis's inner defenses, pounding them with some one hundred heavy guns. It was more than Cornwallis could take. At about nine o'clock on the morning of October 17, the guns fell silent. A white flag was seen above the enemy's works.

Thirty minutes later, Washington received a message that read: "Sir, I propose a cessation of hostilities for twenty-four hours, and that two officers may be appointed by each side, to meet at Mr. Moore's house to settle terms for the surrender of the posts at York and Gloucester. I have the honor to be, etc. Cornwallis."

America had never seen anything like it. The two armies were lined up two deep on each side of the road leading out of Yorktown. On the right were the French, resplendent in their white uniforms, plumed hats, and black gaiters.

On the left were the American Continentals, rigid in assorted ragged hunting jackets, most of white cloth. And, standing in their assigned place, were the militia, soldier-farmers, and others wearing their own clothes.

The allied lines stretched away from Yorktown for half a mile. At the far end, Washington, Rochambeau, and de Barras sat their horses and waited for their defeated enemies to approach. Grouped behind the commanders were their aides and top officers.

Precisely at two o'clock, as Washington had demanded, the conquered British and Hessians appeared in their bright uniforms and polished boots. At the insistent beat of drums and the sad melody of "The World Upside Down," played by the army band, the column moved slowly forward.

The officer leading the enemy troops, however, was not Cornwallis. When he reached the French high command at the end of the line, he asked, "Be so kind as to point out General Rochambeau, please."

"General Washington is our commander in chief," came the reply. "He is there on the right."

The officer immediately turned and approached Washington. "I am Brigadier General Charles O'Hara," he said. "I am acting on behalf of General Cornwallis, who is ill." Then, with a brisk movement, he drew his sword and offered it to Washington, handle first.

Since O'Hara was of lower rank, Washington refused it and said calmly, "General Lincoln on my right will accept."

Unruffled, O'Hara handed the sword to Lincoln, who had only recently been returned to the Americans in a prisoner exchange. Lincoln brought the ceremony to a close by directing some eight

Under Washington's watchful eye, British Brigadier General Charles O'Hara surrendered to General Benjamin Lincoln.

thousand of Cornwallis's force to an area encircled by French troops.

"There, by divisions," he barked, "you are to deposit your arms!"

For Washington, it was a satisfactory close to a long, difficult, and arduous campaign. But, Yorktown, he knew, did not mean the end of the war.

By the first week of November, 1781, the allies were ready to quit Yorktown, scene of one of the most important victories of the war. The Americans and their booty and supplies were on board ships readying to sail to Head of Elk. And prisoners were loaded aboard a variety of vessels to be shipped to secure areas. Rochambeau's troops, however, would remain in Virginia.

Finally, there were farewell dinners and the exchange of gifts, including two horses that Washington presented to de Grasse.

On November 5, Washington and his staff rode out of Yorktown. Along the route to Mount Vernon, Washington was met by a messenger who carried ominous news: "Jacky Custis is ill and asking for you," he was told.

"What's wrong with him?" Washington asked in alarm.

"Camp fever," was the grim reply.

"Where is he?"

"At his aunt's home in Eltham."

"Does his mother know?"

"She's on her way."

With crisp orders, Washington sent his entourage on to Mount Vernon. He then put his horse to the gallop toward Eltham, Virginia. Several hours after his stepfather arrived, Jacky Custis died.

After the surrender, Jacky Custis had left Washington's camp abruptly, saying only that he was going home. On the way, however, he became so ill that he decided to stop at the Burwell Bassett's in Eltham, home of his mother's late sister.

Martha and Jacky's wife, Nelly, arrived at the Bassett's ahead of Washington. While both women were grief-stricken by Jacky's sudden demise, Martha was hit especially hard. She had, after all, lost four children fathered by her first husband, Daniel Custis. Two of the children had died at childbirth; the third, Patsy, died in 1773 while still very young. Then, too, she was saddened by the fact that she and George had no children of their own.

Resolutely, Washington remained to make the funeral arrangements and comfort Martha and Nelly. And when it was all over five days later, he asked her, "What do you want to do? Do you want to stay with Nelly awhile? Or do you want to come to Mount Vernon with me?"

"Since Nelly has the children and the rest of the family to keep her occupied, she doesn't need me," Martha answered in a low voice. "You do."

Then, as an afterthought, she asked, "Don't you?"

"Yes," he said with a smile and a hug, "I do."

$\mathcal{A}$fter four months of conferring with Congress in Philadelphia, Washington moved the army to Newburgh, New York, where he established Headquarters for a possible campaign in 1782.

As the enemy was quiet, he urged Martha to join him. While life was always more bearable when she was near, he also thought their being together at a new place would help keep her mind off the loss of Jacky. Their home this time was another stone house high up on the banks of the Hudson with a marvelous view to the east.

As the days rolled by, there were these developments:

- Benedict Arnold and his family moved to England.
- Henry Clinton had been recalled to England and was replaced in New York by Sir Guy Carleton, longtime commander of British forces in Canada.
- Admiral George Rodney defeated and captured de Grasse in a huge sea battle in the West Indies.
- A small French fleet sailed into Boston harbor, but was bottled up by British Admiral Samuel Hood.

- Congress asked the states for the right to collect customs duties. Unfortunately this could not happen until the states amended the Articles of Confederation, which had been adopted by Congress late in 1777, but not ratified until March of 1781.
- Lafayette returned to France.
- Washington spent much of his time plotting a series of "what if" campaigns; plans that filled twenty-two pages. He also labored to keep the army busy and content.
- He gave his officers long furloughs.
- He asked that every tent be tastefully decorated and fronted by an arbor made of the branches of trees to create shade.
- He issued new hats, which he suggested ought to be given "a military and uniform appearance by cutting, cocking, or adding such other decorations as the soldiers think proper," and he approved the wearing of chevrons on the sleeves and jackets and coats for enlisted men; one for each year of service.
- He advocated daily drills accompanied by music, and urged attendance at religious services on Sunday.
- Finally, he established the army's first "Badge of Military Merit" for privates and noncommissioned officers. It was, he said, to be issued for ". . . instances of unusual gallantry" and "extraordinary fidelity and essential services in any way."

The badge, he said, should be worn on the left breast and should be shaped as "the figure of a heart in purple cloth or silk." With this decoration, the ordinary soldiers who wore it could pass all guards and sentinels, giving them the same privilege as officers. This would show that "the road to glory in a Patriot army and a free country is thus open to all." Eventually, the Purple Heart became available to every deserving soldier.

As the year waned, Washington was saddened to learn that John Laurens had died while fighting off a British foraging party in North Carolina. At about the same time, he also received a report that Charles Lee had died. In October, Horatio Gates returned to the army. Congress had repealed the order that he be investigated for his conduct at Camden.

Three months later, Rochambeau and his troops left for Santo Domingo in the Caribbean. Meanwhile, Nathanael Greene sent word that the enemy was about to evacuate Charleston.

Across the Atlantic, peace negotiations were under way. But while military operations had ceased in the now independent American Colonies, the British remained at their posts in New York City and elsewhere. This caused Washington to wonder whether Britain would again turn on America once it settled its differences with its European adversaries, principally France.

"I confess I am induced to doubt everything, to suspect everything," he wrote to a friend.

uddenly, Washington faced a new crisis. Through almost all of 1782, not a single state made its required contribution to the financial needs of the army. In fact, Congress collected only $5,500—not even enough to cover the expenses of one day.

Again, the army could not be paid. Again, there was a mutiny; this time by the Connecticut Line. And again, the ringleaders were rounded up and executed.

Now, however, the officers appeared ready to resist authority. Obviously, if that happened, the army would collapse. And so might the peace negotiations going on in France.

The officers hounded Congress to find a solution to this explosive problem. On January 6, 1783, a three-man committee of high-ranking officers met with Congress and presented their grievances, saying: ". . . We have borne all that men can bear. Our property is expended, our private resources are at an end. . . ." There was no mistaking their mood. They meant business.

A panicky Congress immediately pushed the states to ratify the amended Articles of Confederation so that the central government could collect customs duties to back up its paper money; a move that would take a unanimous vote.

Tiny Rhode Island refused to ratify. And Virginia, the largest state, changed its vote from yes to no. This meant there would be no collection of customs duties. Congress, in effect, was bankrupt. The officers would not be paid.

Since Congress was a committee of delegates helpless in its dealings with the thirteen divided states, some believed that Washington should assume leadership of the nation with the backing of the army. In other words, he should become a military dictator.

Among those who advocated such a drastic move was Colonel Lewis Nicola. In a seven-page proposal, Nicola argued that since Washington had led the army through ". . . difficulties apparently unsurmountable by human power," he should become "King" and crowned "George I of the United States."

Washington was outraged. "Be assured, sir," he told Nicola, "no occurrence in the course of the war has given me more painful sensations than your information of there being such ideas existing in the Army [which] I must view with abhorrence and reprehend with severity."

But Nicola's idea refused to die. Even Alexander Hamilton hinted at the possibility. Now in Congress and a member of the "Grand Committee" named to hear the complaints of his army friends, Hamilton pointed out that Congress was not only in debt to the army, but to scores of businessmen, manufacturers, farmers, boat captains, and others. These people also must be paid, he said. "The state of our finances," Hamilton told Washington in February 1783, "was probably never more critical."

The army should push its claims "with moderation but with firmness," Hamilton said. And, he argued, Washington should "take direction" of the army. The army should then work with "all men of sense" to develop a way for the government to tax the public; a step "which alone can do justice to the creditors of the United States."

On the heels of Hamilton's letter came another from Virginia Congressman Joseph Jones, who warned that there were "dangerous combinations in the army [that] are about to declare they will not disband until their demands are complied with."

Public creditors, Washington was also told, were ready to join the army in the field to help collect their money. Would Washington lead the army in what amounted to an armed insurrection against the states?

Early on March 10, a white-faced David Humphreys burst into Washington's office without knocking or speaking and handed his chief two sheets of paper.

In a voice tight with anger, Humphreys said,

"The top sheet is an unsigned circular calling on all officers to attend a meeting tomorrow. The other is another circular that . . . I can't describe it!"

After a quick glance at the first note, Washington began to read the second. He was barely past the first few lines when he jumped to his feet and roared, "No! No!"

This circular, also unsigned, urged the officers to choose one of two alternatives: (1) if the war continued, they should leave their posts, go to a remote area of the country and set up their own government; or (2) if peace came, they should hold on to their arms.

"My God," Washington said. "This clearly advocates mutiny by the officers!"

Later, Washington quickly issued a General Order blasting the attempt to call an unauthorized meeting for "such disorderly proceedings." He then set his own meeting for March 15, four days later. The meeting was to be held in the Temple, a large building at the camp used for church services and dancing parties.

"The senior officer in rank present will be pleased to preside and report the result of the deliberations to the commander in chief," the order read. All regiments were to be represented to discuss how to ". . . attain the just and important object in view."

The order implied that he would not attend the meeting, that Horatio Gates would chair it, and that Washington was interested in his officers' views and would present them to Congress in an orderly manner.

He then let Congress know what had taken place. In an additional note to Hamilton and Congressman Jones, he said he wanted to ". . . arrest on the spot the foot that stood wavering on a tremendous precipice, to prevent the officers from being taken by surprise while the passions were all inflamed, and to rescue them from plunging themselves into a gulf of civil horror from which there might be no receding."

Washington decided to attend the meeting despite a protest from Martha that a hot-headed officer could draw a pistol and kill him.

When he entered the Temple from a side door that opened on the dais where Gates was seated, there were loud murmurs of indignation and resentment. Gates, hiding a smile but saying nothing, rapped for order.

With a nod of the head to Gates as the only preamble, Washington drew a paper from his tunic, cleared his throat, and began to read.

"Gentlemen," he said. "By an anonymous summons, an attempt has been made to convene you together; how inconsistent with the rules of propriety! How unmilitary! And how subversive of all order and discipline." He said the anonymous circular was addressed more to "the feelings and passions than to reason."

It was a long speech, one of the longest that Washington had ever made. Despite the scowling, grim faces, the angry glances, the restless, noisy shifting of feet and chairs, Washington went blithely on, his big voice easily reaching every corner of the hall. He spoke with conviction and a voice often tinged with sadness and strong emotion.

With biting phrases, he castigated the anonymous pamphleteer who had addressed the army a few days earlier. Then he added:

"If my conduct heretofore has not evinced to you that I have been a faithful friend to the Army, my declaration of it at this time would be equally unavailing and improper. But as I was among the first who embarked in the cause of our common country, as I have never left your side . . . as I have been the constant companion and witness of your distresses, and not among the last to feel, and acknowledge your merits. As I have ever considered my own military reputation as inseparably connected with that of the Army; as my heart has ever expanded with joy, when I have heard its praises, and my indignation has arisen, when the mouth of detraction has been opened against it, it can scarcely be supposed, at this late stage of the War, that I am indifferent to its interests."

But how are these interests to be promoted?, he

asked. The anonymous phampleteer suggested, he noted, that the Army should move into "unsettled" areas and leave "an ungrateful country" to defend itself.

"But who are they to defend?" he went on. "Our wives, our children, our Farms, and other property which we leave behind us? Or, in this state of hostile separation, are we to take the two to perish in the Wilderness, with hunger, cold and nakedness?

"If Peace takes place, never sheath your sword, says he, until you have obtained full and ample justice. This dreadful alternative, of either deserting our country in the extremest hour of her distress, or turning our Arms against it . . . has something so shocking in it, that humanity revolts at the idea.

"My God! what can this writer have in view by recommending such measures? Can he be a friend to the Army? Can he be a friend to this country?

"Rather, is he not an insidious Foe? . . . Sowing the seeds of discord and separation between the Civil and Military powers of the Continent?"

Washington conceded there might be some "impropriety" in addressing the officers during their meeting. "[But] if men are to be precluded from offering their sentiments on a matter, which may involve the most serious and alarming consequences that can invite the consideration of mankind, reason is of no use to us. The freedom of speech may be taken away, and, dumb and silent, we may be led, like sheep, to the slaughter."

He said Congress, like all large bodies, moved slowly, but he was convinced it would respond to the needs of the Army with "complete justice."

The officers, he said, could "freely command" his services to attain justice for all their "toils and dangers, and in the gratification of every wish, so far as may be done consistently with the great duty I owe my country."

He ended by asking the officers not to take any steps that would "lessen the dignity and sully the glory" they had already achieved.

Silent and stony-faced, the officers waited and watched as Washington calmly drew another sheet of paper from his tunic. "I have here," he said, "a letter from a member of Congress received just this morning. I would like to read it."

Suddenly, however, Washington seemed confused. Abruptly, searching hands delved into pockets. Out came a pair of eyeglasses. Gingerly, Washington put them in place.

The men nudged each other and murmured loudly in astonishment; they had never seen Washington wear glasses! Noticing their surprise, Washington smiled and said wryly, "Yes, I have not only grown gray . . . but almost blind in the service of my country."

Sighs, moans and tears swept the audience. The truth of that simple statement—so warm and human—wrung every heart. And destroyed every bit of resentment.

Washington quickly read the letter, which was

a pledge of support for the officers. When he finished, he nodded at his audience, nodded at Gates, and left. With his departure, America had survived the most perilous hour in its history.

O n April 19, 1783, Washington told a gathering of his troops in front of the Temple that the war had finally ended. A treaty with England had been signed and ratified by Congress. Now it was time to secure the peace.

In his twelfth "circular" to Congress and the states, Washington said that with the end of hostilities the United States faced the most serious danger of all: disunity.

While assuring Congress that this was the last time he would take "any share in public business," Washington called for "a convention of the people" to "establish a federal constitution." The constitution, he said, would reduce states to the status of counties (subordinate to a central government). State legislatures would take care of local problems. But, when "superior considerations predominate in favor of the whole," local voices "should be heard no more."

In an impassioned plea for the future of the nation, he added: ". . . It is yet to be decided whether the Revolution must ultimately be considered as a blessing or a curse; a blessing or a curse, not in the present age alone, for with our fate will the destiny of unborn millions be involved."

Four things, he said, were essential "to the existence of the United States as an independent power.

"1st. An indissoluble Union of the State under one Federal Head.

"2dly. A sacred regard to public justice.

"3dly. The adoption of a proper peace establishment, and

"4thly. The prevalence of that pacific and friendly disposition among the people of the United State which will induce them to forget their local prejudices and policies, to make those mutual concessions which are requisite to the general prosperity, and in some instances, to sacrifice their individual advantages to the interests of the community."

Lastly, he said that unless the states joined in a "form of government so free and uncorrupted, so happily guarded against the danger of oppression . . . it will be a subject of regret that so much blood and treasure have been lavished to no purpose; that so many sufferings have been encountered without compensation and that so many sacrifices have been made in vain."

This impressive document, which came to be known as "Washington's Legacy," showed that Washington, arguably before anyone else, envisioned the nation that now exists.

Having sent Martha back home with the promise that he would join her in time for Christmas, Washington gathered up what was left of his army and rode to New York astride Old Nelson, entering the city on November 25.

As the column of troops proceeded southward through wildly cheering crowds, they were joined by civilians, many of them former soldiers.

At Fort George at the tip of Manhattan Island, the British had taken down their flag and with it the halyards (guide ropes). They had also greased the flagpole to thwart the raising of an American flag.

But as the British soldiers and sailors watched from their boats in gleeful anticipation, a quick-thinking man found a pair of cleats at a nearby ironmongers and used them to climb the pole and quickly attach the American flag at the top.

With the flag snapping briskly in the strong northwesterly breeze, Henry Knox repeatedly called out "Fire!" In rapid succession, cannons boomed and belched fire and smoke thirteen times; a clear signal that the United States was now totally in American hands.

Before leaving New York to appear before Congress in Annapolis, Washington called his officers together for a farewell luncheon at Fraunces Tavern.

At a teary luncheon at Fraunces Tavern in New York, Washington says good-bye to his officers.

As the officers silently ate their food and drank their wine, they waited for Washington to speak. Finally, glass in hand, he rose and said in a voice choked with emotion, "With a heart full of love and gratitude, I now take leave of you. I most devoutly wish that your later days may be as prosperous and happy as your former ones have been glorious and honorable."

"Hear! Hear!" the officers responded with raised glasses.

The meal over, Washington rose again and with eyes swimming in tears, he said, "I cannot come to each of you, but shall feel obliged if each of you could come and take me by the hand."

Henry Knox was the first to step forward and extend his hand. Weeping openly, Washington threw his arms around Knox, hugged the burly shoulders, and kissed the general on the cheek. As each man came up, he did the same, trying all the while to murmur his heartfelt thanks.

At three o'clock, Washington, without looking back at the silent, teary-eyed officers who lined the street in front of the tavern, walked down the street to the barge that would start him on his way.

Uppermost in his mind was a question: Could he keep his promise to Martha and be home by Christmas?

"Sir, the United States in Congress assembled are prepared to receive your communications."

With these words, Thomas Mifflin, president of Congress, opened the proceedings at noon on December 23 in the Annapolis State House before the delegates and a gallery packed with the city's most eminent citizens.

Washington, who had been seated with aides David Humphreys and Benjamin Walker standing on either side, rose slowly and moved to the center of the chamber to face a small group of delegates, each of whom had his hat on.

Washington bowed. The delegates doffed their hats but did not bow or nod. Washington drew a sheet of paper from his pocket and read the following words:

"Mr. President: The great events on which my resignation depended having at length taken place; I have now the honor of offering my sincere Congratulations to Congress and of presenting myself before them to surrender into their hands the trust committed to me, and to claim the indulgence of retiring from the service of my country.

"Happy in the confirmation of our independence and sovereignty and pleased with the opportunity afforded the United States of becoming a respectable Nation, I resign with satisfaction the Appointment I accepted with diffidence. A diffidence in my abilities to accomplish so arduous a task, which however, was superseded by a confidence in the rectitude of our Cause, the support of the Supreme Power of the Union and the patronage of Heaven.

"The successful termination of the War has verified the most sanguine expectations, and my gratitude for the interposition of Providence, and the assurance I have received from my Countrymen, increases with every review of the momentous Contest.

"While I repeat my obligations to the army in general, I should do injustice to my own feelings not to acknowledge in this place the peculiar services and distinguished merits of the Gentlemen who have been attached to my person during the war."

At the obvious reference to his officers, Washington's voice broke and he was overcome by emotions so strong that he had to steady his papers with both hands so he could continue.

Regaining his composure, he went on: "I consider it an indispensable duty to close this last solemn act of my Official life, by commending the Interests of our dearest Country to the protection of Almighty God, and those who have the superintendence of them, to his holy keeping."

With his audience in tears, and his voice breaking repeatedly, Washington continued: "Having now finished the work assigned me, I retire from the great theater of action; and bidding an Affectionate farewell to this August body under whose orders I have so long acted, I here offer my commission, and take leave of all the employments of public life."

He arrived at Mount Vernon on Christmas Eve.

And as Old Nelson pounded up the drive, there in the doorway to greet him, he found Martha, Nelly, and her children—the children squealing with delight.

 *Important Dates*

1775

May 10	George Washington attends Second Continental Congress in Philadelphia
June 15	Unanimously elected commander in chief of "all the Continental forces"
July 3	Assumes command of some 16,000 men at Cambridge, Massachusetts

1776

March 17	British evacuate Boston
April 4	Washington leaves Cambridge for New York City
June 29	British begin arriving in New York area
August 27	Americans defeated at Battle of Long Island
August 29	Washington moves army from Brooklyn Heights to Manhattan
September 15	Begins long retreat that ends in Pennsylvania in December
December 25–26	Surprises Hessians at Trenton, New Jersey

1777

January 3	Defeats British at Princeton
January 6	Establishes winter quarters in Morristown
July 24	British fleet leaves New York for Philadelphia; Washington, after an

	overland march, arrives in the area ahead of it
July 31	Marquis de Lafayette given rank of major general by Congress; Joins Washington later
September 11	Washington defeated at Brandywine
October 4	Defeated at Germantown, but saves army
December 11	Begins to move troops to Valley Forge

1778

February 6	American ambassadors in Paris sign a treaty of alliance with France
February 23	Baron von Steuben arrives at Valley Forge
June 18	British evacuate Philadelphia; General Howe's replacement, Sir Henry Clinton, starts north through New Jersey
June 28	Washington defeats Clinton at Monmouth Court House despite disobedience by General Charles Lee
July 4	Lee court-martialed, found guilty, and suspended
July 20	Washington establishes Headquarters at White Plains, New York
December 11	Establishes Headquarters at Middlebrook, New Jersey

1779

July 16	Stony Point recaptured
August 19	Powles Hook victory
November 16	Establishes winter Headquarters at Morristown, New Jersey

1780

July 1	Moves army to Hudson Highlands
August 3	Gives Benedict Arnold command at West Point
September 23	Arnold's betrayal revealed with capture of Major André

1781

May 21	Meets French at Wethersfield, Connecticut
August 20	Feints at New York and starts moving south
August 30	Admiral de Grasse blockades Chesapeake at Yorktown
September 24	Siege of Yorktown begins
October 19	Cornwallis surrenders

1782

March 31	Establishes Headquarters at Newburgh, New York

1783

March 15	Gives Newburgh address
May 19	Announces end of war to officers and men
November 2	Gives "farewell orders" to troops
December 4	Says farewell to officers at Fraunces Tavern in New York
December 23	Resigns commission at Annapolis, Maryland, and returns to Mount Vernon

 *Suggestions and Acknowledgments*

For those interested in further reading about George Washington, the main sources of material for this work are recommended. They include a variety of wonderful and important books that are rich in detail, full of interesting characters, anecdotes, and insights, all by leading journalists and historians.

Like *First in War*, most of these books relied heavily on the writings and papers of Washington and others who were somehow involved in the American Revolution.

Among the texts researched for *First in War*, were *The War of the Revolution*, by Christopher Ward; *Patriots—The Men Who Started the American Revolution*, by A. J. Langguth; *Ordeal at Valley Forge*, by John Joseph Stoudt; *George Washington in the American Revolution*, by James Thomas Flexner; *History of the United States*, by George Bancroft; *Washington's Lady*, by Elswyth Thane; *Encyclopedia of the American Revolution*, by Mark W. Boatner III; *The American Revolution*, by Bruce Lancaster; *Washington*, by Douglas Southall Freeman; *Turncoats, Traitors and Heroes*, by John Bakeless; *The Negro in the American Revolution*, by Benjamin Quarles; *The Spirit of Seventy Six*, edited by

Henry Steele Comanger and Richard B. Morris; *Forge of Liberty,* by Leonard Falkner; *The Oxford History of the American People,* by Samuel Eliot Morison; *George Washington,* by W. E. Woodward; *The American Revolution— French Allies,* by Robin McKown; and *The Benjamin Franklin Papers,* by Frank Donovan.

Thanks goes to the staff of the Paoli, Pennsylvania, Library, including director Michele Post and staff members Maggie Smaltz and Carol Troy for their always cheerful and efficient assistance. Other libraries that gave the author considerable help include the Trydefferin Library, the Chester County Library, and the Philadelphia Free Public Library.

The valuable advice and counsel of Sara Landis, a longtime friend and a veteran of the publishing industry, is much appreciated. And, once again, special thanks goes to Millbrook editor Laura Walsh. As with two earlier books, her perceptions, intelligent comments, diligence, and encouragement were invaluable as the labor of producing this volume went forward.

 *About the Author*

This is the second volume in John Rosenburg's three-book series about George Washington. The first, *Young George Washington: The Making of a Hero*, tells the story of Washington's childhood and his involvement in the French and Indian War as a young man. The third will be *First in Peace: George Washington, the Constitution, and the Presidency*. John Rosenburg is also the author of *William Parker: Rebel Without Rights* and several other books. He lives in a suburb of Philadelphia with his wife, Rosemarie.